Therapy with Children

Ethics in Practice series

Ethics in Practice edited by Tim Bond is a series of short,
practical guides to ethical issues which confront
counsellors, psychotherapists and other professionals
every day. Suitable for both students and practitioners,
the books are designed to give a clearer understanding
of issues which are often considered complex
and contentious.

Therapy with Children

Children's rights, confidentiality and the law

Debbie Daniels and Peter Jenkins

SAGE Publications
London • Thousand Oaks • New Delhi

SAGE Publications Ltd
6 Bonhill Street
London EC2A 4PU

SAGE Publications Inc.
2455 Teller Road
Thousand Oaks, California 91320

SAGE Publications India Pvt Ltd
32, M-Block Market
Greater Kailash – I
New Delhi 110 048

British Library Cataloguing in Publication data

A catalogue record for this book is available from the British Library

ISBN 0 7619 5278 0
ISBN 0 7619 5279 9 (pbk)

Library of Congress catalog card number 130168

Typeset by Keystroke, Jacaranda Lodge, Wolverhampton
Printed in Great Britain by Biddles Ltd, Guildford, Surrey

Contents

Legal references: UK

Table of cases

Table of statutes

Foreword

Debbie Daniels and Peter Jenkins approach the complex issue of the rights of children to seek and sustain psychotherapy with skill and sensitivity. They provide a lucid and accurate account of psychoanalytically-oriented counselling and psychotherapy and illustrate how the needs of the child for a place of confidential safety is essential for any child to trust a therapist, and eventually, for the society of 'childhood' at large to appreciate the sanctuary provided by this trust.

The authors take the reader through the history and arguments of statutory legislation and common law decisions which bear on the child's right to therapy. This is an exceptionally important research, which will be of immediate use to therapists and counsellors as well as those in the law and local and national government who struggle day in and day out with the vexing questions of balancing the rights of the child with society's need to protect children who may be in harm's way.

In the heart of the book are several deeply moving examples of the fate of children who sought therapy, but who suffered the unfortunate consequences of understandable but misguided interventions on the parts of social services and the police. What is the actual fate of public intervention in the life of a child who seeks therapy? Although the public may feel assured by vigorous intervention in a child's therapy, mandating the therapist's co-operation with the authorities, does it actually work?

Daniels and Jenkins' book arrives at a crucial moment in the history of the therapeutic treatment of children and adults. It is fair minded, exceptionally informative, well written, and compelling.

Christopher Bollas

Acknowledgements

The start of this book came from a chance telephone discussion about children's rights which transformed a dissertation idea into a book for publication. The original idea for my part began as a dissertation title while I was a student at Regent's College. I would like to thank Alessandra Lemma, my dissertation supervisor at that time for helping me to formulate these ideas in the early stages of writing. Brett Kahr, my tutor and mentor, was also instrumental at that time in encouraging me to transform my experiences into a dissertation and publication, and I am grateful for his support. I would also like to thank head teachers, Alessandra Wilson and Victor Burgess who have trusted my professional judgement to act in the best interest of the child client. Over a period of difficult years in exploring the complex issue of confidentiality when working with children I have been grateful for the opportunity to discuss these ideas with my supervisors. I would therefore like to thank Michael Morice, Caroline Helm and Andrea Sabbadini for their support and interest.

Thanks also to family members, namely my sister Diane, who is a counsellor and has allowed me to use her as a sounding board over the years to thrash out the ideas for the book. My warmest thanks also to my parents-in-law for their constant support and interest in the book and all areas of my professional work. Above all, my most heartfelt thanks go to Tony for his endless love and support and not least of all for his dynamic input in my early struggles with the word processor. Finally, I would like to thank all those children who have been my clients and have taught me that what they really want from a therapeutic encounter is nothing more than to be heard and understood.

DD

Acknowledgements are due to a number of people who have helped to make this project a reality, through their encouragement or more practical forms of help. Ray Woolfe, former tutor at Keele University, and Mary Berry, Senior Lecturer at Manchester University, have both provided much-valued support for writing and research as part of professional development. Tim Bond, of Bristol University, former chair of the British Association of Counselling, has been a source of both critical and supportive editorial comment throughout the project. Former colleagues at Stockport College of Further and Higher Education, including Ralph

Barnett, Fred Wolstenholme, Tina Miller and Peter Smith, have been supportive, as have Stephanie Danziger, Linda Stone, Josie Lee, Khatidja Chantler and Sue Hawkins, together with many students on counselling courses. As always, the College library staff provided essential help with materials and inter-library loans. Current colleagues at the University of Central Lancashire who have shown great interest in this project include Maureen Robinson, Jim Martin, Peter Cardew and Jean Aaron-Walker.

Thanks also to my family, near and far, but particularly Jane, Rachel and Lisa, for creating the space to make this possible.

PJ

Promises, promises
Written by a 12 year old girl

I asked you for help
And you told me you would if I told you the things my
dad did to me
It was really hard for me to say all those things
But you told me to trust you
Then you made me repeat them to fourteen different
strangers.

I asked you for privacy and you sent two police men to
my school
In front of everyone, to go downtown
for a talk in their black and white car
Like I was the one being busted.

I asked you to believe me and you said that you did
Then you questioned me over and over again
And took me to court where lawyers put me on trial
Like I was a liar.
I can't help it if I can't remember times and dates
Or explain why I couldn't tell my mum
Your questions got me confused
My confusion got you suspicious.

I asked you to put an end to the abuse
You put an end to my whole family
You took away my nights of hell
And gave me days of hell instead
You've exchanged my private nightmare
For a very public one.

Taken from a longer poem first published in: Meston, John (1989) 'Child Abuse in Canada', pp. 171–190 in Hepworth, H. Philip: *Canadian Seminar on Childhood Implications for Child Care Policies*, Gananoque, Ontario, Canada, June 29–30, 1988. Vienna: European Centre for Social Welfare Policy and Research.

Part I THEORETICAL FRAMEWORKS

Introduction

This book has grown out of the convergence of two distinct, but over-lapping themes – the enormous therapeutic potential of working with the child as the immediate client in counselling and psychotherapy, and the increasing impact of law and literature on the issue of children's rights. Following a career in education, Debbie Daniels has worked as a counsellor in a number of school settings, both in the UK and abroad. She brings direct experience of trying to negotiate a secure framework for providing children in school with space for a therapeutic relationship. Debbie has a Certificate in Education and an MA in Psychotherapy and Counselling. She is registered as a psychotherapist with the United Kingdom Council for Psychotherapy (UKCP) and adheres to the psychoanalytic approach. Peter Jenkins holds an MA in Counselling, works as a student counsellor on a part-time basis, and has published a wide range of articles on the topic of children's rights and on legal aspects of therapy. The combination of these two approaches sheds light on the many dilemmas facing those counselling children. This book presents case material, anonymised to protect the individual client's identity, and links it to discussion of the issues facing Debbie as the therapist directly involved in each situation. The concerns include key practice and professional issues, the scope and outcome of the therapy involved, and the legal framework and options available to the child, therapist and parents.

This focus on the value of work with the child as the immediate client derives from the pioneering practice of therapists working within the psychoanalytic tradition, therapists such as Melanie Klein, Anna Freud, Donald Winnicott and even, in a more qualified manner, Sigmund Freud himself. This is not to ignore or minimise the important work of later therapists or those working from other approaches, such as the person-centred approach or cognitive behavioural models, but simply to trace the development of the child-focused work back to its roots. The crucial importance most therapists place on confidentiality, boundaries and the maintenance of a secure framework for therapy, derives ultimately from the psychoanalytic tradition. The lasting impact of these principles is developed in the first chapters, as the basis for establishing a working alliance with the child as client for sound therapeutic reasons.

This emphasis on the child as client is not an implied criticism of the behaviour or role of parents, as supposedly unwelcome intruders in therapy with children. In some cases an approach involving parents directly in therapeutic work, such as family therapy, may be called for. Nor is it the case that parents are assumed to be the cause, directly or indirectly, of whatever problems the child is exploring in therapy. This would be no more than an extension of the common process of blame, or *mal de mère*, which locates the ultimate causes of children's behaviour in poor child-rearing practices. The particular case argued here is that effective therapeutic work with the child requires a secure and confidential space for the work to take place. External pressures from parents or other adult authority figures will, it is argued, limit and ultimately undermine the value of whatever work may be carried out.

Some brief explanation of terms is called for. The term 'therapist' is used in a generic sense, to include counsellors, psychotherapists and counselling psychologists. It does not include teachers or social workers, valuable as these roles are in other contexts, unless their primary activity involves contracted therapeutic work with a client. Therapy in this sense is seen as distinct from situations where teachers and social workers may be using counselling or interpersonal skills as an adjunct to, or support for, their primary professional role. Having said that, however, there is much within this book which may be of interest or direct relevance to members of professional groups such as teachers, social workers, nurses and doctors.

The term 'child' is used throughout the book to describe a young person under the age of 18. In reality, much of the therapy covered in the book will relate to young people in their teens, where using the term 'child' may seem rather clumsy or even inappropriate. Despite this possible objection, the term child is used because it carries a specific legal meaning, based on the definition under the Children Act 1989, which refers to a person under the age of majority. It is used throughout in this sense to provide consistency, rather than constantly using the broader and all-inclusive phrase 'children and young people'.

'Children's rights' are at the core of the argument developed here for an approach to therapeutic work which prioritises the needs of the child as client. This term is used to denote where a claim can be made for treatment, either by the child or on their behalf, based on established legal or quasi-legal authority such as an Act of Parliament, international convention, code of practice, case law, or official policy document. A vast and increasingly significant number of rights for children now exist in the UK, or more specifically England and Wales, which need to be brought together and understood by all those working with children as a matter of urgency.

The concept of 'confidentiality' is situated right on the contested borders of therapy and the law. Confidentiality is a strongly held professional responsibility for therapists, based on ethical principles and codes of practice. Therapists learn through their training that client material is to be contained securely within the therapeutic framework, in order to establish the fundamental trust necessary for the work to take place and to promote the client's ability to make autonomous choices. The conflict that arises concerns the requirement or discretion on the therapist's part to break confidentiality, with or without the client's permission. These issues assume a heightened importance in a culture where public and professional awareness of child abuse has grown in the last two decades to become an ever-present background. On occasions, child abuse is a more immediate concern for therapists. The duty to maintain a client's confidence in therapy arises where this would be a legitimate expectation, given the special nature or degree of trust involved in the relationship. However (and this is a major qualification), therapists in England and Wales do not enjoy the sort of privilege which, for example, is held by a solicitor who confers with a client for the purposes of giving legal advice. On the other hand, however, mandatory child abuse reporting laws do not apply to therapists in England and Wales as they do to many of their colleagues in the USA. There are many circumstances in which the therapist's ability to provide confidentiality in work with children is constrained by the law. These situations are outlined in detail in an earlier publication (Jenkins, 1997a) and are further explored here.

The format followed by this book is to set out the necessary theoretical frameworks of law and the psychoanalytic tradition of work with children in the first four chapters. The second half of the book then provides a detailed examination of legal, practice and therapeutic issues raised by specific case studies of therapy with children. The book concludes by considering the need to focus on the issue of empowerment for children.

The authors' shared concern to maintain confidentiality in the therapeutic relationship also has implications for the use of 'live' case material for the purposes of this book. The danger of the client's identity being realised by either the client or by a third party is one that is, unfortunately, seemingly inherent in the use of realistic case material. This requires particular vigilance on the part of the therapist in disguising identifying features of the client. Freud recognised this problem in his earliest work: 'It would be a grave breach of confidence to publish material of this kind, with the risk of patients being recognized and their acquaintances becoming informed of facts which were confided only to the physician' (Breuer and Freud, 1985/1991: 47). Every effort has been made, therefore, to avoid any inadvertent breaches of confidentiality through this same process of 'deductive disclosure', by changing key identifying features of the child's characteristics and situation.

Securing a safe framework for confidential therapeutic work with the child as client needs to be based on full knowledge of the relevant law, as opposed to convenient or ill-founded assumption. In working therapeutically with children, as with adult clients, therapists will increasingly discover that ignorance of the law is no defence. This book is intended, therefore, to provide a background of information and discussion which will hopefully promote safe and effective therapy with children.

1

Children's rights: from dependence to autonomy

This chapter looks at some of the historical background to the issue of children's rights. Children have been subject to widespread forms of restraint and subjected to arbitrary authority by adults in the past, and continue to suffer this in many parts of the world today. It is only comparatively recently – during the last hundred years – that children have been afforded rights of protection in the UK. The process of conferring rights on children gathered pace during the twentieth century, with the development of children's entitlement to services providing them with health, education and protection from abuse in the community. The recognition of the child's right to express their views and have these views considered by adults is much more recent still, as a development which has mainly taken place since the mid-1970s. Clearly, acknowledgement of children's growing involvement in decision making and their access to a fuller range of civil rights needs to be qualified by obviously limiting factors such as their age, level of understanding, and degree of physical and emotional vulnerability. However, the automatic, unthinking adult stance of rejecting this growing degree of entitlement is increasingly hard to sustain, due to a wider appreciation that there are different *levels* of decision making rather than it being an all-or-nothing issue. There have also been shifts in legal thinking on this topic, which recognise children's competence as being linked to their level of maturity and understanding rather than simply being related to a fixed chronological age. This approach is endorsed by findings about children's ability to handle apparently complex dilemmas regarding health care and to express considered views on difficult decisions in court settings. This historical background is, therefore, necessary to place in context the debate about children's specific rights to confidentiality and to partnership within the therapy, a debate which is developed in the chapters that follow.

History of childhood

Childhood is frequently presented in terms of romantic and idealised images. The reality of childhood for many of the world's children, both now and in the past, is often very different. On a global scale, children continue to die at the rate of 30,000 a day from preventable causes (UNICEF, 1993: 57). In the Western world, children may be protected in terms of immediate threats to their health but the scale of other threats to their well-being, such as physical and sexual abuse, has been a growing concern during the 1980s and 1990s. According to commentators such as De Mause, far from being a rosy experience, 'the history of childhood is a nightmare from which we have only recently begun to awake' (De Mause, 1991: 1). His psychogenic theory of history, which suggests that parent–child relations are an independent source of historical change, may not be entirely persuasive. However, his approach identifies distinct modes of child-rearing which have held sway at different historical periods. His views are useful in challenging any temptation to see childhood and the status of children from an unquestioningly optimistic and progressive perspective. He identifies the major child-rearing modes as including the infanticidal, abandonment, ambivalent, intrusive, socialisation, and helping modes.

Infanticidal mode. This mode of child-rearing was widespread in Ancient Greece and Rome, particularly with regard to female children, or children with a perceived disability. Children are killed or disposed of to limit family size or manage population growth and to restrict the numbers of 'undesirable' children, that is those who are female, have a disability or who are otherwise judged to be unacceptable in some way.

Abandonment mode. This mode includes the policy of severing the parent–child bond, through sending children to be brought up or fostered elsewhere – with the children holding the status of hostages, pages or servants. It also covers the practice of sending very young children for 'wet-nursing', described as 'the form of institutionalised abandonment most prevalent in the past' (De Mause, 1991: 34).

Ambivalent mode. The ambivalent mode of child-rearing relies on the popular metaphor of children as being pliable: open to control through a variety of measures. De Mause refers to the popular imagery of the 'physical moulding of children, who were seen as soft wax, plaster or clay to be beaten into shape' (1991: 51). Children in this mode of child-rearing are thought of as raw material for adults to shape according to their own moral values and preferences.

Intrusive mode. Control over children is here exercised through direct physical methods, including threats, punishment, beatings, and through the use of psychological domination – such as inducing guilt, for example over masturbation – as an internalised form of social and individual control.

Socialisation mode. Relying on psychological theories, both from a behavioural background (for example Skinner and Watson) and those from a psychodynamic perspective (such as Freud and Bowlby), the emphasis here is much more on training the child in socially desirable behaviour and in guiding the child, often through the medium of 'sound advice' to parents from apparent experts (Hardyment, 1983).

Helping mode. This child-rearing mode rests on an acknowledgement of the child as an active participant in the process of growing up. According to this approach, perhaps best exemplified by Dr Spock, the 'helping mode involves the proposition that the child knows better than the parent what it wants at each stage of its life, and fully involves both parents in the child's life as they work to empathise with and fulfil its expanding and particular needs' (De Mause, 1991: 52).

The question of *power* in the relationship of children to parents and caregivers is crucial here, as elsewhere, in determining the credence given to the child's voice in adult discussions. De Mause charts a historical movement from children's overwhelming dependence and vulnerability, towards achieving increasing degrees of autonomy, within what remains a fundamentally adult-centred society. His argument, that these modes of parent–child relationships are an independent source of social change, overlooks the degree to which family relationships reflect other types of change, such as economic progress, the development of mass communications and the changing position of women in society. However, his overall conclusion is striking, namely that 'the further back in history one goes, the lower the level of child care, and the more likely children are to be killed, abandoned, beaten, terrorized and sexually abused' (De Mause, 1991: 1).

His use of a historical or developmental perspective may, however, be overstated. Infanticidal and abandonment modes of child-rearing are not safely confined to past history, but continue to operate today in large parts of the world. A case in point concerns the difference between natural and actual survival rates of male and female children in certain parts of the developing world; 'In Bangladesh, India and Pakistan it adds up to more than a million deaths every year. In other words, a million girls die each year because they are born female' (UNICEF, 1992: 57). It may be more useful to see the child-rearing modes described above as relating to different ways of perceiving children, which can still be identified in various situations around the world today, rather than as describing a linear, progressive evolution towards a more ideal, child-centred society.

Children's rights

The concept of children having rights of their own is a relatively recent one in historical terms. A 'right' is here defined as a claim to treatment, according to law or policy; a 'child' is defined as a person under the age of 18 years, as per the Children Act 1989.

Opponents of the concept of children's rights have usually focused on the emotional, physical or intellectual immaturity of children as simple, deciding factors in the debate. Evelyn Waugh, for example, dismissed children simply as merely being 'defective adults' (MacDonald, 1998: 4). D.H. Lawrence, no traditionalist in other respects, argued:

> We've got to educate our children. Which means, we've got to decide for them: day after day, year after year, we've got to go on deciding for our children. It's not the slightest use asking little Jimmy 'What would you like, dear?' because little Jimmy doesn't know. And if he thinks he knows, it's only because, as a rule, he's got some fatal little idea into his head. (Lawrence in Berger, 1974)

Children have, for centuries, been seen as mere possessions of their parents, with no entitlement to rights of their own. This conception was a cornerstone of the law in England and Wales for centuries and included the parental right of chastisement – even extending it to include the power of life or death, according to one judicial authority writing in 1706.

> If a parent or master be provoked to a degree of passion by some miscarriage of the child or servant, and the parent or master shall proceed to correct the child or servant with a moderate weapon, and shall by chance give him an unlucky stroke so as to kill him, that is but a misadventure. (Jones, 1945: 10)

If children were seen as possessions, they were also often perceived as having less value than domestic or farm animals. Freeman illustrates this by reporting the case of a woman sentenced in 1761 to two years' imprisonment for putting out the eyes of young children, in order to take them around the country for the purposes of begging. Tellingly, Freeman writes, 'To have done this to sheep could have entailed the death penalty' (1983: 15). Perhaps also significantly, from this point of view, the Royal Society for the Prevention of Cruelty to Animals (RSPCA) was established in 1840, while the National Society for the Prevention of Cruelty to Children (NSPCC) was not set up in England until 1882. In a revealing statement Mundella, sponsor of an 1889 Act to prevent cruelty to children, claimed that he was 'anxious that we should give children almost the same protection that we give . . . domestic animals' (Freeman, 1989: 129).

The status of children as possessions or property was closely linked to the inferior position of women in Victorian society. It was automatic, up to the 1840s, for children to be given into the custody of their father in the case of divorce or separation. Under the Custody of Infants Act 1839, the Court of Chancery became able to grant custody of a child under the age of 7 to the mother. In making the decision, the question of the 'fitness' of the parent was the main concern. It was only in 1873 that the mother's right to custody was extended to children up to the age of 16 years (Thane, 1981: 19).

During the twentieth century, the view that children do possess rights gained ground. At a minimum these children's rights include rights to health, welfare and protection, but were carefully gauged so as not to intrude upon the foundation rights of parents or the basic patriarchal rights of the father to ownership and control of his children. Thus, the growing debate about the extent of child poverty and the extremes of neglect and abuse by some adults led to pressures for a change in the law to enable the Poor Law Authorities and voluntary organisations to intervene to protect children suffering abuse or neglect. Even then, the degree of reluctance to intervene was considerable. Lord Shaftesbury, speaking on the extent of child cruelty, remarked that 'the evils you state are enormous and indisputable, but they are of so private, internal and domestic character as to be beyond the reach of legislation' (Freeman, 1989: 130). This defence of parental privilege found a contrary response from Gerry, a reformer in the United States, who claimed that 'children have some rights, which even parents are bound to respect' (Freeman, 1989: 129).

At the heart of this debate about welfare rights for children was the concept of the patriarchal authority held by the father, restated in law in the *Agar-Ellis* wardship case in 1883:

> the Court must not be tempted to interfere with the natural order and course of family life, the very basis of which is the authority of the father, except it be in those special cases in which the state is called upon for reasons of urgency, to set aside the parental authority to intervene for itself. (House of Commons, 1984)

The beginnings of significant inroads into the rights of parents came with a set of legislation passed in the late Victorian period. This legislation authorised emergency intervention by the state and voluntary organisations, such as Barnado's (then Dr Barnado's), to protect children from neglect. This form of intervention steadily gathered pace during the twentieth century, with a growing range of legal powers for social workers to protect children, entitlement to free primary and secondary education, and health promotion under the National Health Service. This interventionist or 'welfare' orientation towards children's rights reached its high water mark in the mid-1980s, with the expression of the view that 'the state has an overriding responsibility to protect children and ensure satisfaction of their basic needs if those caring for them are failing to do so' (House of Commons, 1984: xiv). Since then, with the so-called rolling back of the frontiers of the welfare state, the contract between state and family has been recast in terms of 'partnership', as illustrated in the Guidance to the Children Act 1989 (Department of Health, 1991a: 3).

Children have increasingly been seen to have rights and preferences which are distinct from those of their parents in the case of divorce proceedings. Lord Denning claimed that the parents' automatic claim to custody of their child actually represented a 'dwindling right which the court will hesitate to enforce against the wishes of the child and the more so the older he is' (*Hewer* v. *Bryant* [1970]). Absolute parental right in divorce cases was no longer to be the deciding factor: parental power 'starts with a right of control and ends with little more than advice'. In other words, children were acknowledged to have their own view in divorce cases, and to have rights and needs set apart from the often conflicting viewpoints expressed by their parents. Children from about 12 years of age could be asked their views by judges in chambers, that is outside the more formal and imposing setting of the courtroom. Indeed, Sir John Balcombe, Lord Justice of Appeal, expressed a clear opinion on this issue: 'I am more and more convinced that even comparatively young children frequently have firm and sensible views to which we should pay attention; certainly no-one . . . should ever refuse to listen to the voice of the child who asks to be heard' (Carolin, 1995: 207). This development is paralleled by the proposal, in the review of adoption law, that consent for the adoption would be necessary from any child aged 12 years capable of giving consent (Department of Health/Welsh Office, 1996: Clause 45).

For children in the local authority residential care system, professionals were long seen to be the experts best qualified to make decisions on their behalf. However, the case involving Maria Colwell demonstrated that there are flaws in such a closed system of decision making, where the child has no right to a voice or to representation within the decision-making process. Maria, aged 7 years, was returned home against her wishes to live with her mother and stepfather, despite having formed a close and affectionate bond with the foster parents with whom she had lived for six years. The child's keen wish to remain with her foster parents, shown by her frequent running back to her foster parents, was not directly presented to the court. Instead, the magistrates were persuaded by the social worker's view that her permanent return home was 'in the child's best interests'. Maria was subjected to persistent neglect when back living with her own family, and her stepfather was later convicted of her manslaughter (Reder et al., 1993: 153). The Children Act 1975 was directly influenced by the press outcry and by the findings of the subsequent Inquiry Report. The Act made direct provision for the child's own wishes and feelings to be taken into consideration in decisions made by the courts and by local authorities, under what was termed the 'welfare principle'. Children were also to be given the right of separate representation through the provision of a *guardian ad litem*, or social worker appointed by the court, to represent the child's interests – as distinct from the case presented by the local authority social services department.

Social work practice was repeatedly under scrutiny from the media, and via official inquiries in the period following the death of Maria Colwell, despite the adoption of closer interdisciplinary cooperation between health, education, social services and the police on the issue of child protection. Media interest reached a new pitch with the situation that developed in Cleveland in 1987, when 121 children were taken into care by social services following concerns that the children were being physically or sexually abused. Professional opinions were sharply divided between social services and medical practitioners on the one side, and the police and media on the other (Bell, 1988; Richardson and Bacon, 1991). The report of the inquiry into these events (known as the *Cleveland Report*) was critical of the apparent breakdown of communication between the agencies involved and of the tendency of the professionals to act on behalf of children, without attempting to involve children in some part of the decision-making process. Noting that the best interest of the child may well conflict with that of parents in the case of investigating sexual abuse, the *Cleveland Report* concluded with a statement of the need to respect the right of children to a degree of participation. Otherwise, 'there is a danger that in looking to the welfare of children believed to be the victims of sexual abuse the children themselves may be overlooked. The child is a person and not an object of concern' (Butler-Sloss, 1988: 245).

The *Cleveland Report* influenced the shaping of the Children Act 1989 in emphasising the need for children to be involved in decision making. This is not to assume, however, that their expressed wishes would always be dominant – an abused child might wish to return home, for example, back to an abusing or unsafe environment, on the strength of an attachment which bonded the child to abusing parents. The *Cleveland Report* also made important recommendations about limiting confidentiality where child abuse was suspected: 'Professionals should not make promises which cannot be kept to a child, and in the light of possible court proceedings should not promise to a child that what is said in confidence can be kept in confidence' (Butler-Sloss, 1988: 245).

As has been noted, the influence of the *Cleveland Report* can be seen in the shaping of the Children Act 1989. Described by its author Lord Mackay (as Lord Chancellor) as 'the most comprehensive and far-reaching reform of child care law which has come before Parliament in living memory' (*Hansard*, 1989), the Children Act 1989 represented a major shift in child care policy, away from state intervention in family life towards a concept of partnership with families and caregivers. Significantly, the notion of parental rights was replaced by the wider concept of 'parental responsibility', defined by Lord Mackay as 'the responsibility for caring and raising the child to a properly developed adult both physically and morally' (*Hansard*, 1989). Parental rights, as distinct from the Victorian approach where the child was seen as a possession, particularly of the father, are now much more closely qualified. Parenthood brings duties and responsibilities, rather than simply the privileges of ownership and control. Contact with separated parents, for example, is seen as a right of the child, rather than simply being considered by the courts as a question of parental access.

The Children Act 1989 endorsed and strengthened the welfare principle, whereby the child's own wishes and feelings need to be considered by the local authority in making decisions; it also confirmed children's rights to be accommodated near to home, together with brothers and sisters if possible. The child's right to respect for their cultural identity is also acknowledged. Following *Cleveland*, the child can express a preference for a male or female doctor, if a medical examination is to be carried out. In addition, the Act enshrined good professional practice in social work, making this the gold standard to be applied to all work carried out by social workers with families and children.

The Children Act 1989 is often thought to apply automatically to all children under the age of 18; in fact, the Act is specifically addressed primarily to local authorities and their departments, in order to produce a corporate response regarding best policy and practice in serving 'children in need'. This is a specific targeted group of children, defined in terms of disadvantage or disability, rather than relating to children in general. The welfare principle applies narrowly to children who are in care or who are being accommodated by the local authority. The concept of the child's welfare being paramount is addressed to *courts* in their decision making – not to local authorities and not to society as a whole. The important principles of the Children Act 1989, therefore, need to be read closely in terms of meaning and context to appreciate their impact upon closely defined groups of children, rather than being assumed to apply widely throughout society.

This is not to understate the importance of the Children Act 1989 as a significant development in the field of children's rights, but to attempt to place it in its proper context. In the field of private law – as distinct from public law which regulates the workings of local authorities and public bodies – the Act has introduced reforms which do speak to the needs of wider groups of children. Under Section 8 orders, for example, children can seek leave of the court to apply for orders determining such key aspects of their life as residence, contact, prohibited steps (e.g. changing school), and any specific issue (medical or other treatment). Section 8 orders made by the court are subject to the 'welfare checklist', which includes reference to 'the ascertainable wishes and feelings of the child concerned (considered in the light of his age and understanding)'. In addition, Section 8 orders may be applied for by a child, given leave by the court to do so (Allen, 1992: 41). Despite media concerns that the Act would unleash a wave of children seeking a 'divorce' from their parents, along the lines of several highly publicised cases in the USA, the numbers of children who have brought these or other proceedings under the Act continue to be numbered in dozens rather than thousands (Bainham, 1994; Houghton-James, 1994).

As part of a parallel global dynamic on the world stage, children's rights have also been highlighted in the international arena. Initially modelled from a welfare perspective, children's rights to protection and to basic health and education have been agreed by international bodies such as the League of Nations in 1924, and again by the United Nations in 1959. Following a ten-year process of discussion, the United Nations agreed the Convention on the Rights of the Child in 1989, now ratified by almost every country on the planet (Jenkins, 1995). This goes beyond the standard claims for provision of health, education and welfare, and for protection from exploitation and disease, in making a new claim for *participation*. Article 12 of the Convention calls for children to be afforded the right to take part in decisions affecting the child, 'the views of the child being given due weight in accordance with the age and maturity of the child' (UNICEF, 1989: 6).

Such participation by children and young people in decision making is far from being a straightforward process to put into practice. All too often the negative assumptions being made by adults will significantly limit the actual involvement of children and young people in the decisions being made. The different types of active or passive involvement being offered are clarified by the concept of a 'ladder of participation', devised by Sherry Arnstein (1969) and then adapted by Roger Hart (1992).

The ladder of participation describes eight levels of children's involvement in decision making, starting from where they are manipulated (level 1), or simply used as 'decoration' (level 2), perhaps for a political or educational event, but without being offered any real understanding of the issues involved. Tokenism, as another level of non-participation (level 3), will similarly occur where children are perhaps approached for their views, but are constrained in the way that their opinions can be voiced or unsure of whether their views can actually have any impact on the eventual outcome. As distinct from this, children can be assigned and informed (level 4); that is, adults may decide on the actual issue, and children can choose whether they wish to take part. Consultation takes this process a step further (level 5); children are actively approached for their views, which are then taken seriously. Adults may also initiate a process, and then share the planning and decision-making with children at every step (level 6). The real autonomy of children begins to develop when children have the initial idea, and decide how they want it to take shape (level 7). Adults are available, but do not take charge of the process. At the highest level of participation, children are fully in charge: initiating, planning and making their own decisions (level 8). Adults are involved here in a supportive capacity only.

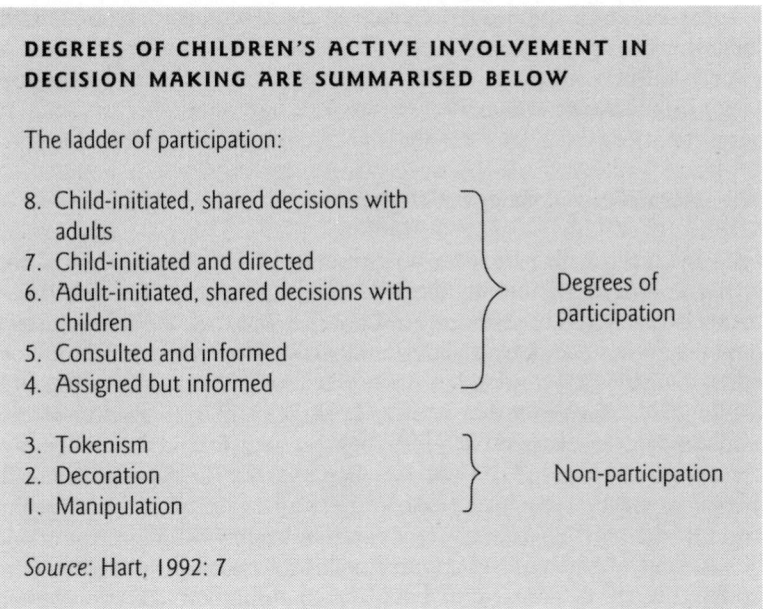

DEGREES OF CHILDREN'S ACTIVE INVOLVEMENT IN DECISION MAKING ARE SUMMARISED BELOW

The ladder of participation:

8. Child-initiated, shared decisions with adults
7. Child-initiated and directed
6. Adult-initiated, shared decisions with children
5. Consulted and informed
4. Assigned but informed

} Degrees of participation

3. Tokenism
2. Decoration
1. Manipulation

} Non-participation

Source: Hart, 1992: 7

Separating out the different levels of participation in this way can allay some of the fears held by adults (and even by young people themselves) that participation in decision making is an all-or-nothing affair – either the child has no say or they are suddenly held to be totally responsible, in the same way that an adult might be. This graduated approach also makes it harder for opponents of children's participation simply to dismiss the involvement of children, on the grounds that young people are unsuited to make complex decisions and, therefore, can be excluded from the widest range of discussion and activity. This attitude was evident in the kinds of argument adopted by the then Conservative Government, in arguing against the extension of the participative principles of the Children Act 1989 into legislation affecting schools. Debating the Education Bill in the House of Commons, Mr Bowis MP rejected the idea that children's views in schools could be considered in a school's decision making.

> The new clause will lead to a gridlock in the management of schools. One cannot have a school in which every decision affecting each child has to be considered by that child, although, having regard to age and understanding, children aged three, four, five or six should be able to toddle into whichever study the decision will be made and be asked, 'Right, Fred, now what do you think?' That situation drifts into the absurd. (*Hansard*, 1993)

The argument constructs children's participation in absolute terms and then conveniently dismisses it as 'dotty' – either each child, regardless of age, is asked their opinion individually or there is no participation at all. Examining the process of participation in terms of levels begins to move away from such unhelpful absolute alternative categories, to explore the real possibilities of participation that may be uncovered.

The *Gillick* case and children's autonomy

For some time, the law has been moving away from a view of children and young people acquiring set rights at fixed ages, as though maturity is inextricably linked to chronological age. This process was given further impetus during the debate about children's right to independent confidential medical treatment. Victoria Gillick sought an assurance from her local Health Authority that none of her five daughters, aged under 16, would receive contraceptive advice or treatment from a doctor without her clear knowledge and consent. Her view was that any doctor giving such advice would be breaching her own rights as a parent to care for her child in the most appropriate manner. The doctor would, furthermore, be assisting a breach of the criminal law if they were encouraging a girl under the age of consent to have sexual intercourse. Her view was supported by two of the Law Lords. They presented a view in defence of parental rights and of the undesirability of children being treated as being prematurely capable of adult decision making. In the words of Lord Templeman: 'There are many things which a girl of 16 needs to practise, but sex is not one of them'. However, Victoria Gillick's case was rejected, in a decision which provided crucial recognition of children's rights – a right to be acknowledged as being independent of their parents. In finding in favour of the then Department of Health and Social Security, Lord Scarman said:

> The common law has never treated (parental) rights as sovereign or beyond review and control. Nor has our law ever treated the child as other than a person with capacities and rights recognised by law. Parental rights are derived from parental duty and exist only so long as they are needed for the protection of the person and property of the child. (*Gillick* v. *West Norfolk AHA* [1985] at 420)

This reshaping of the concept of parental rights is clearly evident in the Children Act 1989, and can be seen in the reframed concept of 'parental responsibility': parental rights only exist as an acceptable and meaningful concept in promoting the perceived welfare of the child. Lord Scarman pared the historic notion of parental rights down to the three limited areas of providing for the child's maintenance, protection and education. Specific parental responsibilities and authority are identified in the box below (adapted from Stainton Rogers and Roche, 1994: 45–6)

Parental responsibilities:

- for the physical care and control of the child;
- to maintain the child;
- to ensure the child receives an efficient, full-time education, suited to his needs and abilities.

Parental authority:

- to discipline the child, using no more than 'reasonable chastisement';
- to consent to medical examination of the child;
- to consent to the child being adopted, or married if over 16;
- to remove the child from the UK.

Based on this list, parental responsibilities and authority may be much narrower than therapists and others assume to be the case. Certainly, a therapist's commitment to the child's rights, for instance to confidentiality, will mean little in practice without an informed understanding of the likely *limits* to their rights and to the actual *remit* of parental responsibility. The most difficult issues arise where the rights of the child and parental responsibility are in conflict. One useful example is where the parent's authority, under the common law, to discipline their child using 'reasonable chastisement' is counterbalanced by the child's right to protection from 'significant harm', under the Children Act 1989 and by the European Convention on Human Rights. In another situation, the child's assumed right to refuse consent to urgent medical treatment for anorexia nervosa will conflict with the parent's wish to authorise the necessary life-saving medical and therapeutic treatment. Knowing the full extent and actual limitations of parental responsibility is crucial if therapists are to offer an informed and professionally accountable service to children (see Chapter 5 for further discussion).

In a situation such as seeking medical advice or contraceptive information, there may well be a degree of conflict of interest between child and parent. According to the *Gillick* decision, the test would be based on the child's level of understanding and their ability to give informed consent. Lord Scarman proposed that:

> the parental right to determine whether or not their minor child below the age of 16 will have medical treatment terminates if and when the child achieves a sufficient understanding and intelligence to enable him to understand fully what is proposed. (*Gillick* v. *West Norfolk AHA* [1986] at 423)

The *Gillick* decision, therefore, has major implications for advancing children's rights to independent choice and decision making, not least in terms of access to confidentiality and to full participant status in a therapeutic relationship – as will be argued in later chapters. With the necessary proviso that it is an adult who decides whether the child is of 'mature understanding', the child or young person is then recognised as being capable of handling complex choices and of making decisions in sensitive areas of their own life.

The *Gillick* decision, while clearly influential in relation to the framing of the Children Act 1989, holds the limited status of case law. It has been challenged by later decisions appearing to weaken its authority in cases of life-threatening or emergency medical treatment for young people (see Chapter 8). However, the *Gillick* decision does not stand alone and is paralleled by similar developments in Scottish statute. The Age of Legal Capacity (Scotland) Act 1991 states that young people of or above the age of 16 years are able to enter into legal transactions, with some exceptions. A young person can give their consent to an adoption order from the age of 12. The basic tenets of *Gillick* are formalised into statute in Scottish law, under s. 2(4):

> A person under the age of 16 years shall have legal capacity to consent on his own behalf to any surgical, medical or dental procedure or treatment where, in the opinion of a qualified medical practitioner attending him, he is capable of understanding the nature and possible consequences of the procedure or treatment. (Age of Legal Capacity (Scotland) Act 1991)

In addition, the Children (Scotland) Act 1995 formalises the principle of children's participation in decision making in s. 6:

> A person shall, in reaching any major decision which involves his fulfilling a parental responsibility . . . or his exercising a parental right . . . have regard so far as practicable to the views (if he wishes to express them) of the child concerned, taking account of the child's age and maturity . . . and without prejudice to the generality of this subsection, a child of twelve years of age or more shall be presumed to be of sufficient age and maturity to form a view.

Given what can best be described as uncertainty about the application of the *Gillick* principle in some situations in England and Wales, Scottish law provides a healthy counterpoint in terms of its clarity and directness.

Gillick and therapeutic work

Adults may be faced with serious dilemmas posed in implementing the *Gillick* principle in relation to therapeutic work with children and young people. In the absence of clear statutory authority, it can seem that counsellors and therapists have to make their own decisions about a child's level of maturity and understanding simply via a rule of thumb, with no proper yardstick to guide them. Therapists working in this area need to have a good understanding of children's cognitive ability and development in terms of decision-making capacity. Downey (1996) provides a brief overview of the different therapeutic needs of children according to age and stage of development, from early school years (4–7 years), late middle childhood (8–12 years) and adolescence (13–18 years). Jezzard (1994) further outlines some of the familiar problems facing any therapist attempting to develop rapport with uncommunicative teenagers.

One practical framework, described as 'Developmental Counselling and Therapy' (DCT), is advanced by Ivey and Ivey. This model is based on the work of Piaget and Kohlberg, which sets out the developmental stages of a child's cognitive ability, and their capacity to make reasoned moral statements and decisions. DCT provides an example of applying a Piagetian framework within a counselling context. 'DCT shows how to identify and assess varying cognitive developmental levels (sensori-motor, concrete, formal, post-formal) as they appear in the here and now of the clinical interview' (Ivey and Ivey, 1990: 299).

The model can be used in a number of ways. Part of the use of the model is in assessing the client's level of cognitive functioning, in order to match the counsellor's responses to the appropriate level of understanding conveyed by the child. Another may be to help the child as client to move onto other levels as seems appropriate.

The different levels of understanding and communication which may be used by the child can include those in Table 1.1. This model may not be appropriate for, or useful to, every therapist working with children. However, using this framework may help the therapist to judge how best to communicate with the child in therapy, in terms of whether to use communication mainly about direct experiences ('What did you do after that?'), or to engage in more abstract exploration of thoughts, feelings and behaviours ('Why do you think this happened to you?'). The authors, working in a US context with children aged 12–13 years, make the suggestion that 'younger children will generally discuss their problems at the sensori-motor or concrete level. Some fifth graders and sixth graders may be expected to operate at the formal level. Relatively few individuals (children or adults) will talk about their issues at the post-formal dialectic/ systemic level unless assisted by the counselor' (ibid.: 301). From a therapeutic point of view, it is not implied that higher levels are necessarily 'better' than lower levels. For instance, a child capable of more abstract thinking may well need to talk about direct physical and emotional experiences, such as feeling angry, in order to make sense of them and then to be able to move on.

The child's level of understanding needs to be assessed on an individual basis by the therapist. Some adolescents may have difficulties with formal or abstract thinking, as indeed do many adults. Children under the age of

Table 1.1 *Using the developmental counselling and therapy model*

Child's stage of cognitive development	Possible responses by therapist	Features of child–therapist communication
Sensori-motor	What has the child seen/ heard/felt?	Communication may be focused on what the child describes as direct, immediate and often random experiences.
Concrete operations	What would be a specific example of this situation? What happened next?	The child's experience may be communicated here in terms of very concrete examples, extending to possible causes of these events.
Formal operations	Where else has this happened to you? How did this affect you (or other people)?	Communication may cover patterns of behaviour/ personal reflections/sense of self.
Post-formal/dialectic/ systemic	How do you make sense of all of this?	This may include exploration of the wider social context/ more sophisticated level of understanding of event.

Source: Ivey and Ivey, 1990

10 have been found to be less competent than adults in their ability to process information about medical treatment, for example (Weithorn and Campbell, 1982). Formal operational thought, the most adult form of reasoning, begins at about the age of 12, and is consolidated in adolescence (Ginsburg and Opper, 1969). This would include some ability to weigh alternatives, and to imagine possible outcomes, both necessary to give meaningful consent for therapy to take place.

The research about children's participation in making health care choices on the basis of the *Gillick* decision is relevant here, given the parallels to be made concerning the need for informed consent and the dilemmas facing professionals about what weight to give the child's own preferences. Perhaps surprisingly, research into children's involvement in health care decision making uncovered significant inconsistencies among caregivers. 'Each adult's view about competence seemed determined less by training or logic than by a disposition to trust or control children' (Alderson and Montgomery, 1996: 47). On the question of children's autonomy, it seems that values, attitudes and gut-feelings are undoubtedly more influential than intellectual arguments or research data. In exploring children's capacity to give informed consent to paediatric orthopaedic surgery, the researchers found that children of different ages could make reasoned judgements about the benefits or disadvantages of having surgery or take part in managing their own pain relief.

The research into a sample of 120 children making health care choices, excluding life-saving treatment, looked at the differing perceptions of the age at which children became competent to make their own decisions. The resulting variation in 'threshold' ages for making decisions is interesting. 'The children themselves set the highest threshold age for self determination at 14 years; the parents put it slightly lower at 13.9 years; and, remarkably, the health professionals chose the lowest figure, 10.3 years' (Shield and Baum, 1994: 1183; see also Alderson, 1993: 9).

The researchers, Alderson and Montgomery, suggest specific areas of health care choices which should *not* be open to the child to decide. These areas include where the child is diagnosed as having a mental illness, such as a psychotic condition; where the choice has irrevocable consequences, as in affecting future reproductive capacity; and where the immediate result of the choice would be life-threatening, as refusing an urgently needed blood transfusion. With these necessary exceptions, they challenge the dominant assumption that children can take part in decision making only in a tokenistic manner. Their work is supported by Pearce, in exploring the child's capacity to give informed consent to psychiatric care. He argues that 'children around 14 years of age are normally able to grasp the more subtle and wider aspects of giving consent, and the effect that this might have on themselves and other people' (1994: 713).

The focus on relative ages of children for being judged to be competent to give consent is helpful, but this approach may draw attention away from the *Gillick* principle, which proposes that evidence of 'mature understanding' is the appropriate criterion rather than age per se. Pearce describes some of the key characteristics of such understanding to be assessed by the professional:

> Competent children will have an ability to understand the nature of their disorder and know why treatment is deemed to be necessary. They should be able to understand the significance of the risks and benefits of having or not having the treatment. In addition, the competent child will be able to understand these issues in relation to the passage of time and be fully aware of what might happen in the future as a result of having or forgoing the treatment. (1994: 714)

These issues will be further explored with regard to therapy in the following chapters, but these comments stand here to underline the importance of the *Gillick* principle with regard to the child's developing autonomy in making decisions.

Summary

The history of childhood has been a bleak and often harrowing one for many children. Long seen as possessions of parents, ordinary children in this country have only comparatively recently won the right to state protection from physical abuse, notably during the last hundred years. The right of children to influence adult decision making is more recent still, developing within social work law, and finding fullest expression in the Children Act 1989 and the United Nations Convention on the Rights of the Child. The powerful concept of 'parental rights' has also undergone a corresponding gradual decline, although its ghost still carries a certain resonance in current discussions about parental authority and control – perhaps more so than should be the case. The *Gillick* decision has continued the wider social trend towards recognising the capacity of children to make informed and intelligent decisions about their own lives. As a key statement of the rights of children of 'mature understanding' to confidential medical advice and treatment, it finds additional support from parallel developments in Scottish statute. *Gillick* opens the door to independent therapeutic work with the child, although the process of judging the child's level of understanding and their capacity to give informed consent remains a problematic judgement for therapists to make. However, it lays the legal basis for working with the child as client, rather than as an adjunct of the wider family group. In therapeutic terms, the necessary complementary foundation for such work has been painstakingly built up by the work of child therapists, particularly those working within the psychoanalytic tradition; therapy with children and the psychoanalytic tradition are the focus of Chapter 2.

2

Therapy with children: the psychoanalytic tradition

Anne Alvarez, a leading child psychoanalyst, states that 'few people now doubt that experiences in childhood and infancy are of fundamental importance in understanding a person's current life and play some part in shaping how he will meet his future' (1992: 1). This view is now so much taken for granted in Western societies, by both lay people and professionals, that it is hard to grasp that before the turn of the century this was a relatively unknown and unexplored concept. Attitudes toward child-rearing practice had improved, if slowly, at least in terms of the child's physical environment. Yet there had been no fundamental understanding that children also have *emotional* needs; there was no real recognition that, psychologically, childhood experiences could indeed influence adult life. The starting point for this discovery came through the psychoanalytic work of Sigmund Freud, although his name may not be the first that comes to mind when thinking about child psychotherapy. Freud's name is more often associated with his work with adults, most particularly with female clients who presented with hysterical symptoms. Yet, it was through this work that Freud was to gain crucial insight into the psychological development of the child.

Between 1892 and 1895, Freud replaced his earlier method of the use of hypnosis with the technique of free association. Patients were instructed to talk freely, and without censorship, about whatever they were thinking. Freud had already discovered that patients frequently avoided talking about painful memories; such avoidance he had given the name 'resistance'. In listening to the free flow of his patients' thoughts, Freud was influenced by the knowledge he had gained from his medical and scientific background, which held high regard for the principle of causal determination. Thus, Freud suggested that the presenting symptoms of his adults may have their roots in childhood. From this, he deduced that it was the painful 'repressed' memories from childhood which had produced symptoms in the adult life of his patients. Freud discovered that patients' memories did not go back just to the time when their symptom began, or to the traumatic event that may have been responsible, but, 'The memories kept going back and back into childhood' (Jones, 1964: 219–20). From a sample of 18 cases, Freud initially thought he had discovered that these patients had experienced some form of what he termed 'rape' or 'violation' in their childhood. Later in life, any normal sexual activity threatened to revive the memory of the childhood abuse and formed a symptom. If the child had been passive in the sexual act, this would lead to hysteria. If the child had been an active participant, this would later form a neurotic symptom. In 1896 Freud gave a lecture on his discovery entitled, 'The Aetiology of Hysteria' (Freud, S. 1896/1966) to the Society of Psychiatry and Neurology in Vienna. The lecture was not well received, and provoked the sceptical comment from Krafft-Ebing, 'it sounds like a scientific fairy tale' (Masson, 1985b: 184).

A year later Freud retracted his theory, saying he no longer believed in his 'neurotica'. There has been considerable debate about why Freud made this retraction. Critics, such as Masson (1985a), claim that it was primarily because Freud had become unpopular and ostracised from psychiatric circles, which to some extent was true. However, Freud's scientific background is relevant here. Freud began to hold serious doubts that, in all of his 18 cases, every patient had experienced sexual abuse in early childhood. In addition, at that time, the techniques of psychoanalysis were only beginning to develop. While having abandoned hypnosis, Freud was still using methods of suggestion; thus, when patients insisted that the scenes they reproduced were not memories, Freud claimed they were in denial. In a much misguided judgement, Freud concluded that the denial meant that the acts in the memories must have actually taken place. He was later to acknowledge that his patients had not been in denial but that it was most probable such events had *not* taken place. In 1914 Freud stated that, 'analysis has led back to these infantile sexual traumas by the right path, and yet they were not true' (1914/1986: 7). Freud was to realise, however, that if hysterical patients could trace their symptoms back to traumas which were fictitious, then a new possibility emerged, which was that they created these scenes in phantasy.

In 1897, the year in which Freud retracted his trauma theory, he embarked upon his self-analysis; as Jones states, it 'is hard for us nowadays to imagine how momentous an achievement this was' (1964: 276). Freud's self-analysis led to the discovery of his own Oedipus complex. In a letter to his colleague Fleiss, dated October 1897, he wrote about the love for one parent and jealous hostility toward the other, giving as an example the legend of Oedipus. The Oedipus complex gave new meaning to the childhood phantasies of his neurotic patients, and to the development of a new theory. In 1909 Freud was able to gain greater insight into his theory on the Oedipus complex in his study of a five-year-old boy, which he called 'The Case of Little Hans' (Freud, S. 1909/1977). This was the first case study which involved the psychoanalysis of a child. Freud was also able to gain greater insight into the powerful phantasy life of children, a phenomenon that he had underestimated during the work on his first trauma theory. This became the basis of his eventual theory outlining the psychology of childhood.

In addition to his clinical contributions, Freud was a proponent of two strongly held views which would greatly assist in the advancement of psychoanalysis in general and which would be particularly helpful in the advancement of child psychoanalysis. The first view was that women should be encouraged to join the psychoanalytic profession. Contrary to the widely held view of Freud as an unreconstructed misogynist, this approach was instrumental in raising the status of women as psychoanalytic practitioners in the wider professional community. The examples of Melanie Klein and Anna Freud, both lay people, gave a powerful impulse to this process of recognition. Freud's related argument was that lay people who were not medically trained should be encouraged to join the profession. It was of particular interest to Freud to enable his daughter, Anna, to gain professional status, but this was not the sole motive for his views. Freud saw that his discoveries in the field of psychoanalysis could filter through to all areas of society. It was, therefore, important for the ideas of psychoanalysis to achieve influence outside and beyond a narrow professional grouping restricted solely to medical practitioners. His theories would then influence areas such as the history of human evolution, children's upbringing and education, and social institutions such as marriage and the law (Jones, 1964: 581). Freud clarified his views in his 1926 publication, 'The Question of Lay Analysis'. Freud's own patient, Joan Riviere, analysed by him in 1922, became the first lay analyst in England. However, the Viennese Society continued to close its doors to lay practitioners. In America the New York Society agreed in 1929 to allow lay analysts to practice, but only to work with children. After the First World War, non-medical practitioners began to work in Vienna, with Otto Rank possibly being the first. Yet Rank was to comment, half-apologetically, to Ernest Jones that 'he only worked with children' (Jones, 1964: 583). A strange notion clearly prevailed in the United States and in Vienna: it was considered that the analysis of children was not as difficult an undertaking as working with adult patients.

In England, child analysis was gaining recognition through the pioneering work of Melanie Klein, herself a lay analyst with no medical training. Psychoanalysis was scrutinised by the British medical profession in 1926, when a committee was appointed to examine its work. In 1929 it was decided that those trained in Freud's methods at the 'Institute of Psycho-Analysis' could be called 'psychoanalysts' (Grosskurth, 1987: 201). In addition, the committee set out certain conditions for training in child psychoanalysis, the first being that 'personal analysis and other stages of training should be the same as for other analysts' (Grosskurth, 1987: 201). Melanie Klein was joined by other female child analysts such as her daughter, Melitta Schmideberg, and Nina Searl. Freud's insistence that women and lay practitioners should be welcomed into the psychoanalytic community did much to enhance the work of psychoanalysis in general and the practice of child psychoanalysis in particular. The Institute currently accepts one third of its trainees from a non-medical background. In addition, the advent of psychotherapy and counselling has enabled lay people to practice in this field, which is now largely dominated by women. Child psychotherapy has thus achieved full professional recognition, after a strugggle reflecting the lower value placed on children as clients compared with adults.

Melanie Klein

Grosskurth, in her detailed account of the life and work of Melanie Klein, states that 'from the moment she read Freud's paper "On Dreams" in 1914 she was enraptured, converted, and dedicated to psychoanalysis' (1987: 3). Living in Budapest, Klein read Freud's work and engaged in her own analysis with Ferenczi. She trained as an analyst in Hungary and Germany, and emigrated to England in 1926. In the 1920s, encouraged by Ferenczi, Klein began to analyse children. The technique of play therapy had already begun in Vienna, through the work of Hermaine Hug-Hellmuth. Yet Klein thought that the latter's work was superficial. She claimed, in her unpublished autobiography of 1957, that Hug-Hellmuth's work avoided interpretations and that there was no analysing of children under six years of age. Klein stated, 'I do not think it too conceited to say that I introduced into Berlin the beginnings of child analysis' (Grosskurth, 1987: 93). Hannah Segal states that Klein was influenced by Freud in her adaptation of play therapy. 'Taking her cue from Freud's (1920) observations of the child's play with the reel, Melanie Klein saw that the child's play could represent symbolically his anxieties and phantasies' (Segal, 1986: 2). Unlike adult patients, young children could not be asked to take an active part in verbal free association. Instead, play was perceived by Klein as a method of free association.

Klein was able to confirm Freud's theories on infantile sexuality, directly through her work with children. In addition, she agreed with Freud's theories on the ego, superego and id. However, her observations in the playroom were leading Klein to formulate her own theories which, by 1934, were beginning to diverge from Freud's original discoveries. First, Klein began by theorising that the Oedipus complex and the superego were in evidence at a far earlier stage than Freud had suggested. Klein observed that with children as young as two there was display of oedipal phantasies and that severely critical superegos were being expressed in their play. Klein traced the formation of both aspects further back to the earliest stages of infancy. Her view was that the Oedipus complex was in evidence in children as young as five or six months old, and that the superego preceded and promoted its development.

Second, Klein examined the various stages in infantile development, which she termed 'positions'. The 'depressive position' was introduced as a concept, in which it was claimed that between the age of six months and twelve months the infant tries to ward off the realisation that he is dependent upon the mother. Following this Klein once more took her thinking back further still, to around the age of four to six months – a stage which she termed the 'paranoid-schizoid position'. In this early stage, gratification through the breast is not always available, and the infant consequently sees the mother as 'good' or 'bad'. In order to cope with the bad breast, the infant splits off and projects an image with a fear of retaliation. The transition from this first position to that of the depressive position is made more easily if there is a predominance of good over bad experiences in terms of upbringing. Eventually a third, healthier, stage is reached – a phase Klein termed 'reparation'. The damage done in the depressive position, in which the infant felt that the mother had been destroyed, is repaired: 'his guilt and despair at having lost her awaken in him the wish to restore and recreate her in order to regain her externally and internally' (Segal, 1986: 92). Klein's contributions to the field of child psychoanalysis were to be further developed, and her key concepts in therapy with children can be summarised as follows.

MELANIE KLEIN: KEY CONCEPTS IN THERAPY WITH CHILDREN

Phases of development:

- Paranoid-schizoid position
- Depressive position
- Reparation

Concepts:

- Part objects
- Whole objects
- Good breast, bad breast
- Splitting and projection
- Envy and jealousy
- Projective identification
- Gratitude
- Manic defence

Clinical contribution:

- Timing of interpretations

Many of Klein's theories were complex and this was reflected in the sometimes rather obscure way in which they were written. For this, Klein came under a good deal of criticism, but she would argue that the theories and writings were only mirroring the complex workings of the child's mind itself. In addition, Klein herself came under attack due to the effects of her often harsh personality and, sometimes, simply because she had branched off from the traditional Freudian approach. Nevertheless, her pioneering contributions to child psychoanalysis were monumental and were increasingly gaining respect and recognition; by 1933, the 'English school' was becoming known as the 'Kleinian school'. Grosskurth, in referring to this period in Klein's life, describes her as 'the cock of the walk'. Freud's former patient, Joan Riviere, and his trusted friend and colleague, Ernest Jones, were both becoming increasingly sympathetic to the Kleinian rather than the Freudian approach. Glover, appraising Klein's 1932 publication *The Psycho-analysis of Children*, stated: 'I have again no hesitation in saying that it constitutes a landmark in analytical literature worthy to rank with some of Freud's own classical contributions'. Klein maintained the unchallenged key position in the area of child psychoanalysis in England until 1938. In June of that year, Freud moved to London with his daughter Anna, Klein's arch rival in child psychoanalysis. Referring to their arrival and the effect on the British Society, Klein remarked to Winnicott: 'it will never be the same again. This is a disaster' (Grosskurth, interview with Clare Winnicott, 1981).

Anna Freud

Anna, the youngest of Freud's six children, was devoted both to her father and to her psychoanalytic work with children. She once remarked that she would not be a good subject for a biography: 'You would say all there is to say in a few sentences – she spent her life with children' (Freud Museum, 1993: 1). Anna began reading her father's work in 1910 at the age of 15. In the early 1920s she began writing papers on psychoanalysis and established her own psychoanalytic practice with children in Vienna. She often worked with children who were deprived through poverty, emotional neglect, or who were separated from their mothers. Unlike Klein, Anna Freud did not feel that the child's play was a form of free association.

> Play with toys, drawing, painting, staging of phantasy games, acting in the transference have been introduced and accepted in place of free association and, *faute de mieux*, child analysts have tried to convince themselves that they are valid substitutes for it. In truth, they are nothing of the kind. (Freud, A., 1966: 29)

She found that, while there were parallels between adult and child psychoanalysis, the application of technique could not always be the same. The instruction to adult patients that they could free associate, and that anything they said would be acceptable, would produce uncensored thoughts with a sexual content. The same instruction to children in the playroom, that anything was acceptable, led to the release of aggressive rather than sexual phantasies, in which children would hit, kick and spit, performing aggressive acts towards objects in the room and often towards the therapist. Nevertheless, Anna Freud maintained that the aim of child psychoanalysis remained the same, to reach the child's unconscious material, even if the absence of free association and the child's acting out made this technically difficult.

In addition, Anna Freud felt that a fundamental difference in treating children as opposed to adults, was that younger children had no understanding of their difficulties and, therefore, no desire in that respect to change. In any event, they would change through a natural process of maturation. She thus stated that 'where pathology is not too severe, the child analyst will query after the successful conclusion of treatment how much of the improvement he can claim as outcome of his therapeutic measures and how much he must ascribe to maturation and to spontaneous developmental moves' (Freud, A., 1966: 28). The 'normal' process of development in childhood thus became a focal point of Anna Freud's work. As children could not assess their own difficulties, she felt it was important for the therapist to make some assessment, differentiating between normal and abnormal behaviour. This led Anna Freud to construct her theories on the developmental lines, those stages of normal growth in which the child develops from a position of dependency to emotional self-reliance. Her theories were outlined in detail in her 1966 publication, *Normality and Pathology in Childhood*. A brief summary follows:

ANNA FREUD: KEY CONCEPTS IN THERAPY WITH CHILDREN

Developmental lines:

1. From suckling to eating
2. Incontinence to adult control
3. Sharing body with mother to own body management
4. Egocentricity to maturity
5. Erotic play to work

Phases of development:

1. The infant needs feeding and is nursed
2. Weaning takes place

3. The child feeds self
4. The child feeds self with utensils
5. Fading out of the equation that food equals mother
6. Fading of sexualization of eating

Initially the environment, most essentially via the mother–child relationship, dominates the child's needs until the child can later satisfy these needs independently. Anna Freud used the term 'phases of development' to describe these interactions.

She applied these theories to her work, as did her colleagues, at the Hampstead Clinic. The clinic was established in 1947 by Anna Freud to serve as a training course in child therapy. (Following her death in 1982, the clinic was re-named the Anna Freud Centre.) Through the establishment of the clinic Anna Freud made a definitive break from the Kleinians in the British Society. This was a decision that followed many years of rivalry and conflict between Anna Freud and Melanie Klein, and between their respective followers.

The Freudian, Kleinian and Independent groups

Anna Freud's father died in 1939, the year following their arrival in London. A relationship of animosity had already formed between the Freuds and Klein; this grew in intensity between Anna Freud and Melanie Klein, threatening to split the British Society unless a resolution could be found. Between 1942 and 1944, against a backdrop of bombs and air raids, a series of talks took place known as the 'Controversial Discussions'. The differences between the Freudian and Kleinian approaches were discussed and heated arguments ensued.

In April 1943, Anna Freud clarified what she perceived to be the fundamental difference between the two approaches. She began by saying that, whereas Klein believed that object relations began soon after birth, she herself maintained that this only took place after the first six months. Thus the infant, rather than loving, hating, desiring, attacking, dismembering its mother, 'is at this time exclusively concerned with his own well-being. The mother is important so far as she serves or disturbs this well-being. She is an instrument of satisfaction or denial, and as such of extreme importance in the child's narcissistic scheme of things' (as recounted in Grosskurth, 1987: 321).

In addition, the Controversial Discussions covered such differences as the dating of the Oedipus complex and the function of the superego. There was also debate about the training provided for analysts. Eventually, a decision was reached in 1946 to form the British Society into two groups, so that trainees could select which approach they wished to follow. Shortly afterwards, it was proposed that a third group be established – a middle group – which later became known as the Independent group. Joseph Sandler stated that, in terms of theory, 'the middle group were always very muddled' (Sandler interviewed by Grosskurth, 1982). Much confusion resulted from the society being formed into various factions, leading Anna Freud to establish her own training facility at the Hampstead Clinic. Nevertheless, the British Society continued to survive, and provide training and practice in child psychotherapy.

Donald Winnicott

With the Freudians and Kleinians in their separate groups, the third influential figure in child psychoanalysis – Donald Winnicott – emerged from the middle group. Winnicott was an ardent supporter of Freudian theory, as he once stated unequivocally: 'let me say at once that I have derived most of my concepts from those of Freud' (1986: 22). Yet, having been in supervision with Klein he was also influenced by her work. He saw both Melanie Klein and Anna Freud as formidable figures and, when the separate groups were established within the British Society, Winnicott joined the middle group. Winnicott had once escaped from his two elder spinster sisters, Violet and Kathleen, by moving from Plymouth to London. Charles Rycroft points out that his escape from his sisters was mirrored when he escaped from Melanie Klein and Anna Freud to join the Independent group (Kahr, 1996: 82). While Winnicott acknowledged that he learnt a great deal from the Freuds and Klein, he also claimed that he learned even more from his direct work with his child patients.

Winnicott began his career as a paediatrician but, unlike his colleagues who all too often concentrated on the child's physical needs, he became sensitive to the emotional needs of children. This interest led him to re-train in psychoanalysis. Winnicott constructed his own theories, some of them having developed from the Kleinian approach. Yet Winnicott's approach was fundamentally different from that of Klein, as Kahr outlines: 'Klein and Winnicott both focused on pre-oedipal aspects of the child's personality, but whereas the former preferred to study the internal phantasy world of the child, the latter concentrated more interest in the actual relationship between child and mother' (1996: 76). Winnicott observed that infants have a need to be loved and to be held, and that anxiety can be created simply by their fear of being dropped. He saw the importance of the use of soft toys as transitional objects when the baby is beginning to separate from the mother. In his analysis of a young girl he called *The Piggle*, Winnicott (1977) dealt sensitively with the emotional effect on the girl of the birth of a younger sibling. His clinical contributions to psychoanalysis were also extensive. Winnicott outlined the reaction of the child therapist in working with severely disturbed children, and whether there could be a psychoanalytic contribution to psychiatric classification. Some of Donald Winnicott's important contributions include:

DONALD WINNITOTT: KEY CONCEPTS IN THERAPY WITH CHILDREN

- The capacity to be alone
- Classification
- Hate in the counter-transference
- The manic defence
- Transitional objects and transitional phenomena

Winnicott was able to apply his theories directly to his extensive work with mothers, their babies and young children. Much of this was undertaken at the Paddington Green Hospital, where Winnicott was a consultant for forty years, and at the London Clinic of Psycho-analysis, where he was in charge of the children's department for twenty-five years. In these situations Winnicott was able to advise mothers on child-rearing practice and to help them to develop close relationships with their infants. Winnicott also worked with evacuees, and stressed the profoundly negative effects which occur when children are separated from their parents. In addition, between 1939 and 1962 Winnicott gave a series of radio talks for the British Broadcasting Corporation (BBC) on child development and child-rearing practice. Subjects included the importance of visiting children in hospital, the contribution of fathers and the psychology of step-parenting. These broadcasts reached millions of listeners.

Freud's hope that psychoanalytic theory would one day filter through to society as a whole, was beginning to be realised, particularly in the area of child rearing. Through the mass media, Winnicott was able to deliver theories on child psychoanalysis to literally millions of parents and educators in each broadcast. Work in the field of child psychoanalysis continued to expand with input from contributors such as John Bowlby, also a member of the Independent group. In the 1930s, Bowlby had studied the disturbances of children raised in institutions and he continued working on the theme of separation after the Second World War. Bowlby supported a colleague, James Robertson, who wished to emphasise the effects of separation from the mother on children who were admitted to hospital. Together they made a film entitled, A *Two-year-old Goes to Hospital*. Bowlby was also interested in the work of Rene Spitz, a Viennese psychoanalyst. Having fled from the Nazis, Spitz moved to Canada where she took a psychiatric post in a prison, working with women who had given birth while incarcerated. Spitz observed that babies left alone for extensive periods in cots on wards would become depressed – some would even die. The effects of separation would be detrimental if the infant was not reunited with its mother within six months. However, Spitz claimed that if the mother and baby were reunited within three months then recovery would be possible.

The observations made by the pioneering child psychoanalysts continue to be applied today in perspectives on child-rearing practice. The direct application of the work carried out by Bowlby and Spitz has led to the current practice of encouraging mothers to stay overnight with their sick children in hospital, while women in prisons are allowed to become involved in the direct nursing and care of their babies. Many of the direct applications of psychoanalytic theory on child-rearing practice have been outlined by Anna Freud (1966: 5–7).

The psychoanalytic approach has provided a major influence on various types of therapeutic work with children. Winnicott's work, for example, has been further developed by that of Dockar-Drysdale, who focused on intensive therapeutic work with 'emotionally frozen' children in residential settings (1993). Erikson's work, based on a Freudian approach, extended Freud's emphasis on the early stages of psycho-sexual development to propose a model which related psychological growth to the process of negotiating transitional changes, such as adolescence (1973). The influence of the psychoanalytic tradition is also evident from more general introductory texts on the topic (Noonan, 1983).

Other approaches to child therapy

Other approaches have also made a significant contribution to an understanding of therapeutic work with children, notably play therapy as developed by Axline (1947, 1973), and by more recent writers such as Wilson et al. (1992) and Cattanach (1995). The work of Alice Miller has been very influential in stressing the need to respect the child as client, and to validate their experiences (1991). Geldard and Geldard (1997) describe the wide range of play therapy techniques which can be used with children from early childhood up to adolescence. Sinason has extended the range of children as clients thought appropriate for therapeutic work through her pioneering work with children with learning disabilities (1992).

The other major influence within therapeutic work with children is that of the cognitive-behavioural school, which has established itself as a viable and effective form of therapy, particularly within school or child psychological service settings (Callias et al., 1992; Downey, 1996). Furthermore, cognitive-behavioural methods have proven effectiveness with regard to specific childhood problem behaviours, such as school phobia and enuresis (Roth et al., 1996: 270; Weisz and Weisz, 1993: 95).

The valuable contribution of other approaches is clearly acknowledged, although the focus of this exploration is primarily on the psychoanalytic approach. This is partly because the psychoanalytic approach is the one which has informed the therapeutic work discussed in the second part of this book, and also because of the particular emphasis within this approach on maintaining therapist–client confidentiality. This is acknowledged by general introductions to therapeutic work with children such as that of Mabey and Sorensen. They discuss the therapeutic importance of the 'maintenance of the frame':

> These boundaries, the elements of the agreed contract that creates the framework and the maintenance of the frame, both confronts the client with the issues that need to be worked on and provides the security for that work to take place. In this respect counsellors from other orientations have a great deal to learn from the psychodynamic approach because much bad practice in counselling results from poor boundaries and frame violations. (Mabey and Sorenson, 1995: 39, cited in Noonan, 1983)

Derived from the psychoanalytic tradition described earlier, confidentiality is stressed as a requirement for effective therapy to take place: hence, 'it is incumbent on the therapist to facilitate the provision of an environment in which the child is permitted free expression' (Harper, 1994: 167). A key distinction within the psychoanalytic tradition is that made between the internal and external worlds of the client. Given this crucial distinction, 'the chief concern of the child psychotherapist is the child's inner world' (Passey, 1994: 173). This clear conceptual separation between the inner and outer worlds, and the exploration of how they interrelate, has contributed to a definite grasp of the need for clear boundaries in therapy with both child and adult clients. Thus, in a section mainly focused on the physical environment, but which could as easily relate to the issue of therapeutic confidentiality, Copley and Forryan argue: 'Despite difficulties in the environment . . . it is important for the worker to hold on to a clearly bounded space for the therapy as an indication of space in her mind for the child, and of a willingness to hold on to and struggle with the thinking' (1997: 31). The factors influencing the therapist's protection of this therapeutic frame or space in working with children are explored in more detail in Chapter 3.

Conclusion

There can be no doubt that, during the twentieth century, psychoanalysis has had a monumental influence on child-rearing practice. In some areas the direct links between psychoanalytic theory and everyday practice can be clearly understood, while in some circumstances the evidence can be more subtle – to the point of being taken for granted. What is clear is that children have benefited in becoming freer in many aspects of their lives and in having society regard them as human beings. The child psycho-analysts afforded children an opportunity to be listened to in a society that had previously favoured the dictum: 'children should be seen and not heard'. A major effect of the psychoanalytic tradition has been in terms of children gaining increasing freedom to express themselves, both within the therapeutic context and within the wider society.

3

Therapy and the rights of the child

This chapter addresses the arguments for considering the child as the primary client in therapeutic work.

Therapists working with children tend to operate from one of four alternative approaches. The first of these advocates the inclusion of parents as active participants in any therapeutic process that the child embarks upon. In the second approach, the practitioner may agree to work with the child as client on an individual basis, but will seek parental permission and may report back to parents. This may take the form either of a general progress report, or through more detailed discussion of the session's actual content. Thirdly, the practitioner initially offers a service based on qualified confidentiality, but may subsequently involve the parents and/or other agencies if it is felt that the child is at risk. The fourth approach is one in which the practitioner offers the child both confidential access to treatment and maintains complete confidentiality throughout the treatment process. These four approaches to confidentiality within therapy with children may be summarised as:

1. Therapeutic work with the family as a whole
2. Parental or adult oversight of therapy
3. Provisional or conditional confidentiality
4. Unqualified or total confidentiality

Such differences in approach depend on two crucial factors. The first is the legal and organisational context of the therapeutic work being carried out. The second, explored in detail in this chapter, depends upon the therapist's perception of the child as either a dependent or independent party in therapy. This perception then determines whether or not parents are to be included within the therapeutic framework. This has long been a point of controversy, one which led Anna Freud to pose the following concerns: 'the issue at stake is a theoretical one, namely, the decision whether and from which point onward a child should cease to be considered as a product and dependent of his family and should be given the status of a separate entity, a psychic structure in its own right' (1966: 43). It is undoubtedly easier to attempt to explore this dilemma from the perspective of the child's *cognitive* development, than from an emotional or developmental one. There are clear-cut definitions in understanding from a cognitive and developmental perspective: when it might be expected that a child can walk, talk, and eventually begin to think in abstract terms along adult lines. The question of at which point a child attains a 'psychic structure' in its own right, however, is not so easily definable and it is of little surprise that this remains a point of controversy.

The theories proposed by the pioneering child psychoanalysts have clearly demonstrated the stages at which the infant and child can be defined psychically as a dependent entity. In focusing on the newborn infant, Melanie Klein outlined her theories on the paranoid/schizoid and depressive stages of infant development. Klein proposed that, during the early months of life, the infant was not only utterly dependent upon the mother but also perceived the mother to be an actual extension of the baby's own self. The level of dependence of the baby upon the mother was further observed by Donald Winnicott through his case work as a child psychoanalyst and paediatrician. Indeed, such was the extent to which Winnicott felt that the infant depended upon the mother that he once announced to the initial surprise of one audience that 'there is no such thing as a baby'. He elaborated on this point some years later, explaining that whenever we encounter a baby, a mother or mother surrogate is always at hand, without whom the baby could not survive, so utterly dependent is the nature of its being. Sigmund Freud (1926) also explored the nature of infantile dependency, and described the period of time in which the infant was helpless and dependent on the mother as the 'biological factor'. During this period, the dependent infant and then the younger child would have a fear of losing the parent and the parent's love, along with a fear of punishment, which he termed as 'educational compliance'. This dependent period was also seen by Freud as responsible for humanising and socialising the child, and for the formation of the child's character and personality, together with their moral and ethical codes.

The dependent period is thus clearly identified, but the beginning of the independent stage appears more gradual and more difficult to appraise. Nevertheless, the dependent period does begin to diminish, as Freud describes it, when the older child begins to fear being disapproved of, not by the parents but by the community – moving from a stage of educational compliance to social compliance. Similarly, Winnicott describes true independence developing when the child is able to live a personal existence that is satisfactory, while involved in society's affairs (1965: 91). Anna Freud advocates some assessment by the therapist to determine the level of independence a child client has attained, through examining how far the child still leans on the parents or to what extent he has outgrown them (1966: 46). In this way it could be observed to what extent the child still identifies with the parents or has begun to build an independent structure. In psychoanalytic terms, the child who has become a separate entity might be able to demonstrate the mastery of ego over id, rather than still being controlled by the parents.

In applying these criteria, we might then encounter children as clients who are able to demonstrate that they are operating from a stance of having developed their own psychic structure. They can, therefore, be considered as separate entities from their parents and family. Alternatively, we may encounter adult clients who still depend largely on their parents for emotional support and constantly seek parental approval for their actions. In some instances, they have never felt able to move away from the family home. Indeed even average adults, as Winnicott states, 'do but seldom reach to full maturity', and he suggests that this only really begins to take place when adults have reached a compromise between copying the parents and defiantly establishing a personal identity (1965: 92). Nevertheless, even in the more extreme circumstances, the therapist of the forty-year-old, emotionally dependent patient would not normally seek permission from the patient's parents to commence treatment or attempt to involve them in the therapeutic process. However, the child client who does present as having attained a level of independence, demonstrating adequate development of the psychic structure, may be denied treatment outright in the absence of parental involvement or consent. Thus the dependent adult is accorded the right to confidential treatment while the independent child is not. However, if we are really applying the concept that the client should not be treated without parental involvement on the basis that the client is not a separate entity, then in view of this criterion the parental involvement for these two clients would actually be reversed.

This is not to suggest there are no psychological or emotional–developmental differences between adults and children. However, those practitioners who adhere to rules on this issue based only on the client's chronological age may be misjudging the client's readiness for, and entitlement to, individual treatment. Perhaps it is more valuable to consider that all clients of whatever age will have reached different stages in their ability to operate as a separate entity from their parents. Winnicott suggests that we think in terms of 'dependence towards independence', for as individuals we are constantly making moves 'towards independence' and do not move directly from one state to the next. In view of this, Winnicott finds it helpful to think in terms of three categories rather than two (1965: 84):

- absolute dependence
- relative dependence
- towards independence

In applying these terms, we might then become more adept in enabling our clients – of whatever age – to move increasingly towards independence for, as it is widely understood and accepted, the basic function of the therapeutic practitioner is primarily to empower the client.

The child's right to confidential access to therapy

How do ideas of childhood dependence influence the practice of therapists? In one case, an inner city school in West London stated in their school policy for the post of student counsellor: 'children are allowed to see the counsellor for one consultation after which parental consent has to be obtained before further sessions can proceed'. On contacting the counsellor at the school to discuss this issue, it became clear that such a ruling dissuaded some students from seeking counselling appointments. Others refrained from attending further appointments after an initial session, where the policy to inform parents had been made clear to them. In addition, it was noted that some parents prevented their children from attending further sessions once they had been informed. However, there was no intention to change the policy for, as the counsellor pointed out, this would be too difficult because they were a 'very family orientated school'. It would seem that the notion that the child cannot be treated as a separate entity certainly prevailed in that particular school. Such a policy may have been admirably attempting to reflect and maintain the unity of family life. Nevertheless, it created a situation in which the school contained any number of troubled students who were not receiving any emotional support, in spite of having an on-site full-time counsellor. Yet the need for the child to have access to confidential treatment is seemingly a growing one, and this has been reflected not least by the advent of the agency 'Childline', which is currently able to deal with 3000 calls per day (although around 10,000 calls a day are actually made to the agency) (*Guardian*, 11 December 1996). Indeed, it could be said that the success of this agency depends to a large extent upon the level of confidentiality offered (see Chapter 4). These figures provide the clearest possible evidence that children desire and need to speak about matters that trouble them, in confidence, and without parental involvement or consent.

Based on personal professional experience in working therapeutically with children in school settings, it became clear that their demand for confidential access to treatment prevailed in the vast majority of cases. Child clients gave various reasons for not wanting their parents to be informed that they were in treatment. These reasons were often based on fear, and conflicted with a perhaps idealised view of parents as protectors and as advocates of their child's well-being. The clearest expression of this came from those children who wished to exclude their parent or parents from the treatment process because the parents themselves were the perpetrators of abuse. In this the child could not depend on the parent or parents to offer protection or to support a process which involved discussion of their questionable parenting methods. Often, in such situations, the family was already known to social services and had participated in family therapy; yet the child had felt too inhibited to talk freely about his or her parents while they were present. In many similar situations, children also sought individual treatment following the breakdown of family therapy where the parent or parents had failed to attend appointments after a few initial sessions, and then denigrated both the process and the professionals involved. The child then preferred to seek out treatment in isolation, not wishing to jeopardise this by informing parents who were known to be suspicious of the process and would perhaps disrupt the child's treatment. The majority of children who sought confidential access to treatment, however, did so because their own parents were unable or unavailable to meet their child's emotional needs. The children felt, nevertheless, that their parents would feel uncomfortable in having their child seek out the help of a professional. Child clients in all of these circumstances had fears that their parents would influence the process in some way or prevent them from continuing treatment.

Such anxieties, as expressed by these children, were not without foundation in external reality. Indeed, child psychotherapists constantly refer to the parental response to their child having treatment as 'parental attacks'. In situations which may involve abuse, but may also simply involve emotional neglect, parents are clearly aware that they may be the subject of discussion in sessions. As child psychiatrists, Tsiantis et al., state: 'the parents can be afraid of the exposure of their inadequacies and/or the family pathology' (1996). They go on to say that 'parents can also be intrusive, trying to manipulate the therapist as they manipulated the child, in response to the feeling of being threatened by the possibility that their defects and faults will be revealed: they will be narcissistically unable to sustain their own emotional balance' (Tsiantis and Anastasopoulos, 1996: 22–3). In addition to attacks on the therapist and on the treatment process from a fear of exposure, there are also recognisable instances of 'envious attacks' towards the child's therapist. Anna Freud describes the parent's feeling of envy occurring at times in which they are aware that the therapeutic relationship is positive, and states that at such times parents might aggravate the loyalty conflict between analyst and parent in the child (1966: 48). Envious feelings appear to be particularly acute in mothers when the therapist is female. Tyson, in her study 'The gender of the analyst', points this out when she says of the mother: 'feelings of inadequacy and jealousy may emerge, and she may feel in competition with the therapist for her child's loyalty' (1980: 321–38).

Such a response has been encountered personally, in varying degrees and on numerous occasions, while working as a therapist. A more moderate attack was posed by a middle class mother, who questioned the headteacher about the duration of her son's treatment, which she complained had 'gone on far too long' after fifteen sessions. Perhaps the most severe case, however, was that of Kay, a white, English adolescent girl who had learning difficulties, whose family had experienced intense emotional difficulties requiring social service interventions over a number of years. Various forms of therapy had been provided in the past, including family therapy and play therapy for the younger siblings. Yet Kay appeared to find her own niche in individual treatment, and remained in therapy for over forty sessions, during which time she improved both emotionally and academically. She eventually terminated her treatment long before it had reached its full conclusion, however, as she could no longer endure the pressure from her mother, who insisted that Kay should break off her treatment and confide her thoughts only within a mother–daughter relationship. Ultimately, her mother continued to remain emotionally unavailable; it was known that Kay's academic performance declined and that there were several reported instances of sexual behaviour in which Kay put herself at appreciable risk. Yet, in addition to an envious attack by the mother towards her daughter's therapist, perhaps something else was also taking place on an unconscious level. During the period of time in which Kay was in treatment, her mother married, and then separated from her fourth husband. She then embarked on a new relationship and found that also to be failing. The younger siblings were reacting to these changes through regressive behaviours such as biting, soiling and smearing faeces. Perhaps in preventing her daughter from continuing in treatment, the mother was fulfilling her own need for Kay to fit into the family dynamic as an ill child. As Anna Freud states, 'some parents, for pathological reasons of their own, seem to need an ill, disturbed, or infantile child and maintain the status quo for that purpose' (1966: 48). In this instance, it may have been too difficult for the mother to endure the fact that Kay's mental health was improving while the rest of the family appeared to be deteriorating.

Parents propose many varied reasons, often containing complex unconscious components, to prevent their children from gaining access to treatment. Yet whatever the situation, in these cases the children involved seemed to have extremely good insight into the manner in which their parents would respond to their treatment – and in most cases asked for confidential access. In some instances, the reasons proposed by children were not very different from those of adult patients. Both adult and child patients said at some point in the future they might inform their parents that they had been in treatment, but only if and when they felt ready to do so. In the meantime, they sought to make use of a private space in which to explore their own thoughts as an individual. In listening to the wishes and anxieties of child clients, it became clear that they needed the same right to confidential access to treatment that was afforded to adult patients.

It became clear, however, that confidential access to treatment would have to depend upon confidentiality being maintained and protected throughout the treatment process.

Child psychotherapy: the psychoanalytic tradition

In examining the issue of confidentiality, the key question is in which circumstances, if any, such a principle should be broken. Advocates of absolute confidentiality, such as Bollas and Sundelson (1995), stand in direct opposition to the mandatory reporting laws concerning child abuse and mental health law in the USA. British professional therapists' organisations, meanwhile, continue to grapple with this complex area, tentatively making suggestions while refraining from advocating any hard and fast rules. However, it would seem that all factions are united in a general belief that confidentiality is a widely accepted – indeed intrinsic – part of the treatment process. Yet it would be remiss to lose sight of how and why confidentiality has become such a crucial aspect of the therapeutic process. While not underestimating the importance of ethical and legal considerations, these are not the fundamental reasons for confidentiality evolving as the core principle of psychoanalysis. In order to understand and fully appreciate the function of confidentiality, we have to return to Freud and the origins of the 'talking cure'.

Freudian psychoanalysis

All present day approaches to counselling and therapy have at their core Freud's basic premise that people can begin to feel better simply by talking about painful past experiences. This is now so widely accepted that we need to be reminded that, before Freud, individuals suffering from symptoms such as hysteria were treated using torturous methods including blood letting, having holes bored into the skull, or being manacled to walls in asylums for the insane (Foucault, 1975). Similarly, it is worth noting that Freud, who is often accused of having been a misogynist (primarily because of his theories on 'penis envy'), was actually the first man to listen, patiently and seriously, to female patients with hysterical symptoms in an attempt to understand the root cause of their symptoms. Before this, women who presented hysterical symptoms were routinely prescribed female circumcisions. Freud thus broke the pattern of former barbaric approaches to those who presented with emotional disorders.

The process of psychoanalysis evolved in the early years of the twentieth century with certain techniques firmly established by around 1915 with the completion of Freud's papers on technique. Freud focused on the use of transference; he sought to understand the mechanism of repression, and to explore the significance of Oedipal enactments and dreams. He encouraged his patients to discuss their uncensored thoughts freely – free association – attempted to bring about changes in the ego structure, and ultimately aimed at making conscious what was once unconscious. As Freud was to discover, however, theories and techniques alone were insufficient to stimulate a process which depended upon the development of an interactive relationship between therapist and patient. For the successful application of such techniques, certain conditions had first to be in place.In 1917, Freud was to state: 'psychoanalytic treatment may be compared with a surgical operation, and may similarly claim to be carried out under arrangements that will be the most favourable for its success' (1973: 512).

A structure thus evolved alongside the techniques and theories which would include the clinical environment, comprising a private room with a couch. The analyst became predictable in manner: always being punctual, adhering to the 'fifty-minute hour', and remaining neutral in providing non-judgemental responses to patient material. In addition, the analyst was to remain an anonymous figure, never indulging in revealing aspects of their own personal life during a session. Most importantly, analysts conducted their work under the prevailing principle of confidentiality. These basic components devised by Freud, when put into practice, established a structure now often referred to as 'the psychotherapeutic framework'. Patrick Casement cites instances from his clinical work in which he unwittingly allowed breaks to occur in this framework, producing difficulties within the sessions (1985: 61–75). The psychotherapeutic framework is, however, perhaps most often associated with Robert Langs, a prominent American psychiatrist and psychoanalyst, who introduced the concept of 'the secure frame'. Indeed, it is in this area that Casement claims to be indebted to Langs for prompting him to 'look more closely into the dimension of the therapeutic relationship' (1985: 71). In keeping with Freudian principles, Robert Langs (1979) outlines the key concepts – the five essential components – of the therapeutic framework:

ROBERT LANGS: KEY CONCEPTS OF THE THERAPEUTIC FRAMEWORK

- Total confidentiality
- Privacy
- Predictability and consistency
- Therapist neutrality
- Therapist anonymity

Each one of these five elements appears to be delicately interwoven with the others. A breach in confidentiality can affect the functioning of the remaining four elements of the framework. This, in turn, can have an adverse effect both on the technical procedure of the process and on the treatment alliance between therapist and client. The negative effects of such a breach are no less profound when working with children than with adults. Indeed, it may be suggested that in some circumstances the effects are actually worse. To understand why this might be so, it is necessary to explore each of these points in relation to therapeutic work with children. As a starting point, however, it is important to note how the concept of confidentiality developed in its own right within the confines of the treatment room. For, to begin with, confidentiality had an immediate bearing upon the success of the technical process known as 'free association'.

Free association

As Freud was to discover, patients continually censor their thoughts or repress important material, because of the anxieties that such thoughts arouse and the restraints imposed upon them through the workings of the superego. Freud therefore encouraged patients freely to discuss whatever thoughts came into their mind, without censorship. This was known as 'free association' or, strictly translated from the German *Freie Einfall*, a free waterfall. In a sense, free association meant letting one's mind dance. Freud (1938) stated that he required 'complete candour' from the patient in the process of free association and, in return, he promised the 'strictest discretion'. In short, it was this pact that set the foundations for confidentiality. Today's adult patient, having formed a similar pact with their therapist, can venture into their unconscious, knowing that the material which is recovered and put into words will safely remain confidential. While it would appear that this fundamental principle of therapy is largely accepted by psychotherapeutic practitioners as being of vital importance, it is not held to in its purest form when working with children. Thus, while the therapist requires complete candour from the child as client, the child is seldom offered total confidentiality in return. Instead, the child is often informed of a general rule of confidentiality and is instructed to talk about anything that comes to mind. Yet quite often, at the same time, the child is given a contrary message that the therapist can give no assurance that certain issues which may arise from their free flowing thoughts will remain confidential. In the normal course of a treatment process, it is known that adult patients will subject their thoughts to repression and censorship, even with confidentiality firmly in place. For the child patient, meanwhile, there can all too often be realistic fears surrounding any attempt to express not only repressed, but even conscious material. For child patients who obligingly and trustingly engage in free association may subsequently find that, due to disclosure by the therapist, they become thrust into court proceedings, removed from or ostracised by their family, or removed from the treatment process entirely – all against their will. Clearly, if the rule of free association is not accompanied by the rule of confidentiality, then the therapeutic work is put at risk.

Therapist neutrality and ego formation

It became clear to Freud that, once repressed material was made conscious, there was not only an expectation from the patient that the therapist would treat such material as confidential, but that he or she would also remain neutral and refrain from making any value judgements about the content. Neutrality is included as an essential component of Langs's therapeutic framework, not only because it is an essential requirement for the process of free association, but also because its continued application eventually alters the structure of the client's ego formation. Freud introduced the concept known as the 'structural model' in 1923, in which he described the functions of the ego and the id. The ego represented what might be called reason and common sense, in contrast to the id which contained the passions. The superego was described by Freud as being that part of the ego responsible for self-criticism and self-observation – and, therefore, the part in which introjected parental images (imagoes) were to be found. It is largely accepted in analytical circles that throughout the psychotherapeutic process the client will begin to project feelings originally held for their parents onto the therapist, through the process known as transference. Yet, by maintaining a neutral stance, the therapist acts as an auxiliary superego, that is, as a non-critical, non-judgemental parental figure (Strachey, 1934: 139–41). Eventually, the client will no longer identify the therapist with his or her own parents and can begin to be freed from their guilt, fears and illusions.

The essential difference in working with children, of course, is that their childhood experiences do not belong solely to the past, but are current in that very moment of time. While both child and adult patients have introjected parental images and voices, for children an additional factor is in operation. In reality the child's parents and parental figures belong, not just to the past, but to the here and now. In examining the history of childhood earlier in the text, it can be seen that children are constantly subjected to the authority of adults in all areas of their lives. Thus, while the adult patient may continue to feel controlled by the introjected parent, the child is frequently controlled by the real parents and by other adults as well. The adult client often encounters difficulties in attempting to absorb the fact that the therapist will maintain a neutral stance, and begins to attain some belief of this only when it has been tried and tested on numerous occasions. Yet it is exceptionally difficult for the child client to accept that the therapist, who is initially perceived as just another adult professional, could offer anything different from other authoritarian adults.

It is hoped that such fears will lessen for the child client, as with adults, through the process of establishing and maintaining a confidential, neutral and non-judgemental therapeutic environment. Yet it would appear that once action has been taken by the therapist to contact outside agencies, as a result of a breach in confidentiality, there is an immediate loss of neutrality. In a sense, the therapist – for whatever positive motives – has made a judgement and has acted upon it. The duty of the therapist is to resist the client's attempts to identify the therapist as the parent. However, it could be suggested that the therapist who makes judgements is no longer perceived as being different from other adults, but is actually seen as belonging to a body of authoritarian figures such as parents, teachers, social workers, police and judges. Thus the therapist who acts as a parental figure no longer represents the auxiliary super-ego, performing an external supportive role, but is instead identified with the client's own super-ego. It is hard to see how the process of transference, the maintenance of the therapeutic alliance, the introjection of a healthy object, or any alteration in the ego structure can then successfully occur.

Therapist anonymity

In addition to neutrality, anonymity was stressed by Freud as playing a vital role in the treatment process. Langs has also included the therapist's anonymity in the five crucial elements of the therapeutic framework. It is accepted by psychoanalytic practitioners that clients should not be informed of details concerning the therapist's personal life or their activities and relationships outside the therapeutic setting. The therapist is then able to maintain a stance known as the 'blank screen', which enables patients to work through the transference concerning their phantasies of the therapist, rather than what is known to be fact.

It is perhaps inevitable that those therapists who make decisions to disclose information about child clients to outside agencies will effectively lose their anonymity. The child who had previously been unaware of the therapist's engagement in external relationships is suddenly all too aware that the therapist is liaising with any number of professionals. In addition, the therapist, who may never have been seen by the child outside the therapeutic setting, may now be observed at (or be known to have attended) case conferences, discussing previously confidential patient material with other professionals – and sometimes even with the child's parents. The child may also witness the therapist giving what had formerly been seen as confidential information as evidence in court. The therapist may be seen reading extracts from case notes in court – notes which the child may have assumed did not exist or, if they did exist, would never become public property. The previously anonymous therapist has now also become a public figure and can no longer represent a blank screen. The therapist is instead perceived by the child as belonging to the authoritarian adult world, and has, as such, become part of the external super-ego structure, which can damage the treatment alliance.

Predictability and consistency

The process of therapy requires precision. It requires the setting up of a structured framework, and demands that the therapist is both predictable and consistent in working within this framework. Not only do the techniques flourish in such conditions, but the client also begins to feel emotionally contained – often for the first time in his or her life. Both adults and children who embark on a therapeutic process will have often experienced a high level of fragmentation and lack of integration throughout their lives. It is, therefore, very important that the therapist does not duplicate the client's external background but instead is able to set up a working environment, and, within that, to provide a series of responses which are both predictable and consistent. The therapist who initially appears to offer the child a confidential relationship and then discards this in favour of disclosure, is breaking a serious ground rule. Langs states that when alterations in ground rules take place, there are several possible consequences for the patient, including an unconscious image and introject of the therapist as someone who is suffering from identity confusion: as one who promises to function as a therapist but fails to do so (1988: 147–8).

It may be suggested that the therapist is indeed suffering from identity confusion in stepping out of the role of therapist into the role of either social worker, police officer or child protector. Clearly, this is not the type of professional that the child had initially chosen to engage with when agreeing to psychotherapeutic treatment; it might, therefore, be reasonable to expect that the child will wish to bring the therapy to an end.

Alternative models

For those practitioners using other approaches to their work, opting for a psychoanalytic model may present certain difficulties. The fundamental difference between psychoanalytic and other approaches lies in the former's belief in unconscious processes, adherence to the structural model, making use of interpretations and holding transference as a central feature of the treatment process. The psychoanalytic model also appears to stand alone with regard to frequency and duration of sessions, usually conducted several times a week, over a period of years. Yet it could be suggested that alternative approaches nevertheless adhere to a similar framework as set out by Langs in key respects. The humanistic or behavioural practitioner also offers the client an environment of privacy, and is predictable and consistent, both in terms of therapeutic practice overall and in offering neutral responses to client material. Perhaps the only significant difference regarding the framework lies in terms of the area of anonymity, in that those therapists working with recovery groups will often disclose their own similar past experiences. Most importantly, practitioners of all approaches adhere to the principle of confidentiality, although their reasons for doing so may differ. The humanistic practitioner may not feel that a breach in confidentiality will have an impact on alterations in the client's ego structure. He or she may, however, feel that the end result of a loss in neutrality, and of the therapist acting upon information, will lead to a breakdown in the therapeutic relationship. Similarly, while the behavioural therapist may have no belief in an unconscious process, and may not use terms such as 'free association', he or she may nevertheless concede that a breach in confidentiality may prohibit the client from talking freely.

The child client may not be concerned about which school of thought the therapist belongs to, but may be concerned that the therapist is predictable, consistent and does not move from being a counsellor to becoming a social worker mid-session. Clearly, at the heart of whatever theoretical model is used, there will be core values and ethical principles which need to be explored and acknowledged in full by the therapist.

Ethical aspects of therapeutic work with children

Ethical issues for therapists are increasingly recognised as a necessary basis for competent and effective practice (Bond, 1993; Dryden, 1997). Rather than simply taking the form of abstract, academic discussion, they represent actual therapeutic dilemmas of a very practical sort. Therapists' organisations have emphasised the role of clear and effective codes of ethics for practitioners, both as an aid to practice and as a key aspect of a wider process of professionalisation. While such codes can give essential information to therapists, supervisors and clients alike, they can often only provide general statements about what is necessary or desirable in facing different ethical problems; it is in the nature of ethical dilemmas that a code of practice, however comprehensive, will not be able to anticipate every situation or offer guidelines for every combination of circumstances (Association of Child Psychotherapists, nd; British Association for

Counselling, 1998b; British Confederation of Psychotherapists, nd; British Psychological Society, 1995; United Kingdom Council for Psychotherapy, 1998).

One useful framework for considering ethical issues in therapy is proposed by Daniluk and Haverkamp (1993) and Thompson (1990). This suggests a model comprising six ethical principles, which can be used to examine and guide practice. These ethical principles include:

- Autonomy: the promotion of the client's freedom of choice and action
- Fidelity: faithfulness, loyalty, the keeping of trust
- Justice: achieving equity, fairness, avoiding discrimination
- Beneficence: doing good, promoting the client's welfare
- Non-maleficence: avoiding harm or damage to the client
- Self-interest: promoting the self-knowledge, self-protection, and self-development of the counsellor

Broad principles like these may be easy to ascribe to in theory but, in specific situations, key ethical principles may well be in conflict with each other. For example, a client's autonomous wish for total confidentiality to be maintained may be at the expense of the client's own welfare, as perceived by the therapist, in the case of a teenager experimenting with potentially dangerous drugs. Applying ethical principles in therapy with children has the additional difficulty applicable to any therapeutic situation where the interests of a third party, such as parents or other siblings, enters into the equation. A therapist may seek to involve parents in the therapeutic work at some level, if only by agreeing to the parents knowing that therapy is actually taking place. The therapist's conscious intention may be to 'do good' (beneficence), by promoting a wider involvement in the therapeutic work. However, the therapist may really be acting out of self-interest, in order to 'cover his or her back' in a potentially difficult situation. The sharing of even basic information with a third party, such as a school teacher or parent, may ultimately be at the expense of the client's autonomy (the therapy may be ended by a third party). Such a breach may also damage the crucial principle of fidelity, as the bond of trust between client and therapist may then be irrevocably broken.

Practical choices by therapists necessarily reflect underlying, and possibly unconsidered, ethical values. Choosing to widen the therapeutic frame to accommodate third parties in work with children will clearly reflect a commitment to certain ethical principles at the expense of others. While no choice of action is perfect, it will be argued with regard to the case examples discussed later that, in many situations, therapist commitment to the child's sense of autonomy is crucial for effective therapy to take place. Promoting the child's self-determination and autonomy is consistent with the central purpose of therapy, and further develops the ability of children to make informed choices for themselves. In some situations, the child's age, lack of understanding or the degree of perceived risk may cause the therapist to override the child's need for autonomy. Here the therapist may act to 'do good', or at least to avoid potential harm, by reporting suspected abuse for instance. However, the therapist who consistently values other principles over the principle of the child's autonomy is offering a narrowly based and restrictive service to their clients. Claiming a lack of knowledge of the law, or conceding to third party demands for access to therapeutic work with children as clients without exploring the ethics of doing so, is in itself a form of unethical practice. Under the principles of self-interest and justice referred to above, therapists have a duty to their clients to be reasonably well informed about the legal basis of their own practice. After all, 'it is incumbent upon all therapists to have sufficient understanding of the legal framework in which they have to operate' (Jezzard, 1994: 197).

The principles referred to above acknowledge that while therapy has a potential to benefit clients, it also holds the possibility of harming their interests or of acting to their disadvantage in some substantial way. Therapists who seek to promote their client's autonomy as a result of uninformed risk-taking, by ignoring potentially harmful situations, or through acting beyond their level of competence or expertise, are clearly not acting to promote their clients' welfare. Therapists need to work within their level of training and competence, and to undergo regular supervision, as a minimum safeguard for protecting the interests of children who are an especially vulnerable clientele.

There are well-documented examples of children experiencing abusive relationships within therapy. These tend to derive from the context of residential care in a social work setting – in part, because this setting is perhaps more open to documentation and to public investigation in the long term than other contexts. In the case of the 'Pindown' regime operated in Staffordshire children's homes in the 1983–1989 period, children were subjected to an oppressive system, alleged to be 'negative behaviour modification', which denied them basic rights such as access to daytime clothing, reading material and contact with parents – even conversation with staff (Levy and Kahan, 1991). According to one critic, 'Pindown provides a salutary example of the dressing up of oppressive control in the rhetorical garb of therapy, and of the capacity of that rhetoric to convince those running the regime that what they were doing was in the best interests of the children' (Fennell, 1992: 312).

A parallel example of abuse of children under the guise of therapeutic work is more pronounced and yet more damaging in the case of the work of Frank Beck. Beck, with minimal training in therapeutic work with children, ran a regime in Leicestershire children's homes during the period of 1973 to 1986. Based on a curious mélange of the work of Dockar-Drysdale, Bettelheim and a Canadian film called *Warrendale*, Beck and his associates developed a form of 'regression therapy' with difficult and disturbed adolescents which came to provide a cover for their systematic humiliation and abuse, both physical and sexual, of the young people and junior staff involved (Kirkwood, 1993). The problematic concept of 'regression', here taken out of its proper context, 'was seized on by Beck to give an apparent theoretical under-pinning for his own "therapies", which used regression, but without any attempt at psychological repair' (D'Arcy and Gosling, 1998: 77).

These two examples of abusive therapy for children and young people illustrate, in a graphic and perhaps extreme manner, the dangers of incompetent and unsupervised therapeutic work which directly damages the physical and psychological well-being of the young clients involved. Therapeutic work with young people in a school, youthwork or private practice setting may come nowhere near offering the opportunities for systematic abuse of children described above. However, the arguments advanced here for confidential therapeutic work with children are meant to be taken in a professional context – with necessary training, supervision and the maintenance of appropriate professional boundaries between clients and therapists being in place. Developing a child-centred form of confidentiality is not a licence for the enthusiastic amateur to provide an unsafe environment for the client, nor is it acceptable for such workers to promise such an environment and then lack the expertise to maintain and safeguard it.

Conclusion

The therapeutic case for working with the child as client has been explored most fully from within the psychoanalytic movement. As in therapy with adults, the maintenance of a secure frame is of critical importance. Working with children can be subject to envious attacks by parents, who may feel threatened by the process of therapy. Yet maintaining confidentiality is at the heart of the treatment process, and to compromise this principle may, in turn, lead to the child losing their confidence in the therapist. Part of the process of developing a safe and effective form of therapeutic practice will require constant reference to the ethical principles spelled out above, to ensure the continued well-being of both client and therapist. As will be argued elsewhere, however, the maintenance of a secure therapeutic frame, and the self-interest of the therapist, also rest on a basic understanding of the legal process as it affects work with children. A knowledge of ethical principles on their own is not enough to carry the therapist and client safely through the maze. Some of the main features of the law which provide the essential context for therapy with children will be explored in Chapter 4.

4

The law relating to therapy with children: contrasting approaches

Many people working with children express uncertainty and confusion about their therapeutic work and the law. Whether practising in a youth centre, school, voluntary agency or other setting, the law seems complex and something of a minefield when it comes to counselling and therapy for children and young people. Do the parents always have to be informed or give permission? Can the young person be offered completely confidential therapy, and if so, at what age? If child abuse is suspected, is it compulsory to report it to the authorities in every case?

Questions like these will confront adults seeking to provide a therapeutic service for young people. The law relating to therapy for adults is complex enough, and the law can appear even more daunting with regard to young people. This chapter sets out some of the main legal boundaries relating to therapy for children (defined as persons under the age of 18, as per the Children Act 1989).

Children's rights

Providing therapy for children as an activity depends, crucially, on an understanding of their rights under the law. There are a number of conflicting approaches to the issue of children's rights (Jenkins, 1993a):

- The 'welfare model': children's interests are decided for them by adults
- The 'participatory model': children have a right to a say in decisions about their well-being
- The 'independence model': children have rights to make their own decisions for themselves

Each of these approaches finds some support under the law. Pastoral care in schools often works on the welfare model, based on the concept of *in loco parentis*, or the school as substitute parent (*Williams* v. *Eady* (1893)). Alternatively, sections of the Children Act 1989 confirm the rights of children to take part in decisions about their future, as for example in discussing whether to return home from residential care. Finally, some aspects of the law, based on the *Gillick* case, stress the rights of children to make certain decisions on their own. Thus children under the age of 16 may be seen to have enough understanding to seek medical treatment or contraceptive advice on their own behalf. The stance taken by therapists will depend upon which model of children's rights they actually support in practice.

Welfare approach to therapeutic work

Under this approach, the child or young person is seen largely in terms of the responsibilities held by adults for their care and protection. Under the concept of *in loco parentis*, the school acts as a substitute parent, with delegated powers of control and authority over the child or young person. Hence, 'the duty of a schoolmaster is to take such care of his boys as a careful father would take of his boys' (*Williams* v. *Eady* (1893)). The degree of quasi-parental authority of the school over its pupils has actually been increased as a result of the educational reforms of the 1980s. As the Children's Legal Centre notes, 'the Education Acts in the 1980s have tended to give increased rights to parents, but this does not necessarily benefit school students' (Children's Legal Centre, 1987: iii). In fact, it is clear in the legislation that *parents*, not pupils, are seen to be the primary consumers of education. While parents have rights to specify their choice of school, to withdraw their children from sex education and to complain about aspects of school policy, the rights of children have been systematically ignored by the changes in the law (Jeffs, 1995). The growth of civil rights for children in the wider society, under the Children Act 1989 and the UN Convention, provides a remarkable contrast with their virtual absence within the school setting (Friel, 1998a).

The effect of this emphasis on parental or adult rights in schools has been to create an atmosphere of uncertainty for those wanting to provide a child-centred therapeutic service in schools. In some school settings, the principle of acting *in loco parentis* may be interpreted in a conservative way, so that counselling may only be provided with the full knowledge and agreement of parents. This may have the effect of deterring many children from approaching the therapist in the first place, or of making them carefully edit what they say if they do take up therapy. In either case, the effectiveness and appeal of the therapeutic service for children may be severely limited as a result.

From one perspective, therapeutic confidentiality in a school setting may be ultimately constrained by the overall responsibility and authority of the head of school. In ethical terms, it would follow that the principle of the child's autonomy is here made secondary to that of beneficence, and the need to protect their perceived welfare, rather than necessarily to promote their right to self-determination.

This responsibility requires the head teacher to exercise judgement over a wide range of issues on school sites including the question of confidentiality for a school counselling service . . . Head teachers have the right to make decisions regarding the sharing of information and confidentiality wherever this is reasonable and in the best interests of the child. (British Association for Counselling, 1998a: 15)

According to this view, therapeutic confidentiality is subject to a wider requirement to comply with the authority of the head of school. Casemore argues that 'no school counsellor employed on teaching conditions of service is legally entitled to keep information about children from the headteacher' (1995: 1). The key phrase here relates to 'employed on teaching conditions of service', which impose a duty to work under the 'reasonable direction' of the headteacher. 'Reasonable direction' might specify that the individual teacher or therapist pass on information about under-age sex, drug use, criminal behaviour, or serious emotional problems, to the head. However, this approach may be more firmly based on custom and practice than on unassailable legal principles. The first school counsellors were originally expected also to teach, and this may well have established assumptions about the limits of their professional autonomy regarding confidentiality which are later hard to deconstruct (Lang, 1999).

From this perspective, the limits to confidentiality are defined by the counsellor's contract of employment, and by the overall authority of the headteacher. However, there is a countervailing argument here concerning the counsellor's fiduciary duty of trust and confidentiality to the child as client (see Chapter 6 for a more detailed discussion of this issue).

Alternatively, a policy of protecting therapeutic confidentiality may be in operation in the school, as negotiated with the headteacher in question. It is possible that a therapist working in a school setting on a self-employed basis may enjoy greater professional autonomy in their work, while remaining accountable for their practice to the headteacher and the school as employer. With delegation of budgets to school level, it is increasingly the case that therapists are employed on a sessional and self-employed basis rather than as full- or part-time direct employees of the school. Counselling services in schools may be provided by school-employed counsellors, the Local Education Authority, an external agency such as the NSPCC, or by a Youth Counselling Service (British Association for Counselling, 1998a). Patterns of confidentiality may vary according to the type of service offered and the nature of the service provider's contract with the school.

It is essential, in any case, that the therapist negotiates very clear agreed boundaries with the responsible school authorities concerning the provision of confidentiality as part of the service on offer to pupils. This may include developing a policy of restricted confidentiality, for example with specific provision for reporting to the headteacher or to social services any instances of child abuse or of potential for self-harm by pupils. However, as argued in Chapter 3, any immediate gains in terms of protecting the welfare of children may well be offset by the inflicting of lasting damage to the 'therapeutic frame' and to the wider credibility of the therapeutic service as seen by those children who are its potential users in the future.

Another concern in school settings relates to counselling young people about issues relating to sexuality. This is partly based on restrictions placed on local authorities regarding the 'promoting' of homosexuality under s. 28, Local Government Act 1988. This section prohibits local authorities from any activity which would 'intentionally promote homosexuality or publish material with the intention of promoting homosexuality', or 'promote the teaching in any maintained school of the acceptability of homosexuality as a pretended family relationship'. This approach was reinforced by Education Circular 11/87, *Sex Education at School* (Department of Education and Science, 1987; since superseded), which outlawed 'teaching which advocates homosexual behaviour, which presents it as the norm, or which encourages homosexual experimentation by pupils'. The effect of this, taken together with other Circulars and legislation, has been to create an atmosphere of risk and uncertainty around issues of sexuality and sex education for those working with young people.

While it is crucial not to blur the key role differences between a teacher carrying out a pastoral role and a therapist working in a school setting, it is still important to identify some of the current concerns and pressures affecting teachers on the broad issue of sex education. These have influenced teachers in terms of their perceived freedom to use counselling skills with their pupils, and in terms of generating a sense of risk and vulnerability in responding to pupils' needs on this issue. This, in turn, can affect the position of therapists seeking to work with children on these or related issues.

In relation to individual counselling or guidance by teachers of young people in school, the impact of successive Circulars has been, arguably, to confuse and heighten uncertainty in an already complex and emotive area. DES Circular 11/87 stated, with regard to giving information or advice on contraception to young people under the age of 16 years: 'the general rule must be that giving an individual pupil advice on such matters without parental knowledge or consent would be an inappropriate exercise of a teacher's professional responsibilities, and could, depending upon the circumstances, amount to a criminal offence' (Department of Education and Science, 1987: para. 26). (This advice is curiously echoed in some counselling texts (Sanders, 1997: 83).) This somewhat alarmist approach is toned down in the later Circular 5/94, *Education Act 1993: Sex Education in Schools* (Department for Education, 1994) which simply states: 'Teachers are not health professionals, and the legal position of a teacher giving advice in such circumstances has never been tested in the courts' (para. 39). The implicit message contained here seems to be that teachers straying over this ill-defined legal boundary would put themselves at risk of hostile legal action by aggrieved parents.

The overall effect of legislation and related media publicity has been to create and maintain an atmosphere of risk and uncertainty for teachers, and, indirectly, for therapists working in school settings. Teachers' and therapists' worries on this score may well be unfounded. A subsequent, little-publicised government circular clearly states that s. 28 'will not prevent the objective discussion of homosexuality in the classroom, nor the counselling of pupils concerned about their sexuality' (Department of Environment, 1988: s. 20).

The confusion generated about sex education in schools and the role of individual counselling on this topic is crucially related to an attempt to limit the positive impact of *Gillick*. The *Gillick* principle is at odds with the parent- and adult-centred ethos of school reform legislation in the 1980s. Circular 11/87 (Department of Education and Science, 1987) was specific in this respect, arguing that the *Gillick* situation of a doctor giving contraceptive advice to young people under the age of 16 had 'no parallel' in the school context. Viewed narrowly, in terms of giving medical advice, this is true. Seen from a broader perspective of the evolution of children's rights, it is actually education legislation which is out of step with wider trends in society and the law. According to Bainham, 'The Education Act 1993 is, frankly, downright inconsistent with the general level of legal autonomy enjoyed by the 16-year-old' (1996: 37).

The restrictive approach surrounding counselling on sex education has developed as a result of the impact of successive circulars. However, the status of the circulars may easily be overestimated. They simply provide guidance rather than acting as authoritative statements on the law, whatever their undeniable impact on shaping policy and practice in schools. Key assumptions embedded in the circulars have also been challenged by independent legal opinion, such as that obtained for the Association of Teachers and Lecturers (Beloff and Mountfield, 1994). This has contested the presumption that criminal and civil liability would arise from teachers giving confidential information on sexual matters to young people in school settings. The likelihood of a criminal offence arising here is seen to be extremely unlikely, where a teacher is seen to be operating in good faith and on the basis of their own professional judgement. Also, the likelihood of action being taken by an aggrieved parent not consulted by the teacher regarding the advice given to their child is also remote, when the basis for any action under the tort of negligence would be hard to establish in any court of law (Bainham, 1996: 29).

Teachers' duty of confidentiality

The critical independent legal opinion discussed above also supports the idea of a space for the teacher using their professional judgement in deciding whether to maintain confidentiality, or to pass on information given to them by a pupil – except in the particular case of child abuse. This area of discretion is now also acknowledged in the area of drug education. Supplementary advice from the Department for Education and Employment (DfEE) to schools on the handling of drug-related incidents states: 'In exceptional circumstances, and in consultation with the relevant agencies, schools may delay the involvement of parents or not involve them' (1998: 36).

Policy under the current Government seems, furthermore, to be shifting towards endorsing this principle of protecting child–teacher confidentiality. A letter from Education Minister, Charles Clarke, to Lord Tope, Liberal Democrat Education spokesperson, is quoted by the *Daily Mail*: 'Schools are not now required to disclose to parents any information which, in their opinion, would cause serious harm to the emotional condition of the pupil' (5 December 1998). This may not carry the status of official guidance, but could be a significant pointer towards the probable direction of development of such a policy. Further guidance on confidentiality in personal, social and health education is to be issued by the DfEE in the near future (DfEE, 1998: 37).

Parents do not, therefore, have an absolute right in law to information given to a teacher by their child; nor can children require that all information be held by a teacher as being absolutely private. Thomson summarises the position:

> The advice from the Department for Education and the Welsh Office does not place an absolute duty on teachers to break confidences, nor is there any legal requirement for teachers to inform parents of matters which a pupil has confided to them. Teachers are, however, bound by their contract of employment. If they are directly instructed by their employer, the head teacher and/or school governors to disclose the confidences of pupils, they could face disciplinary measures if they do not comply. (1996: 107)

This view shifts the onus from the individual teacher to the school management as a whole. Providing therapy in the school setting, as well as meeting the need for effective sex education, requires a policy of confidentiality which respects pupils' autonomy and capacity for decision making, and protects young people from risk. While past legislation and government circulars have appeared to restrict teachers' freedom to act, there is a strong legal case to be made that despite the uncertainty, a role remains for teachers to exercise their own professional judgement about how to handle those confidential disclosures by pupils which do not deal directly with child abuse. This emphasis on the teacher's professional judgement may have implications for therapists in schools or working elsewhere, who are bound by professional standards and codes of ethics (see Chapter 5). This recognition of professional judgement has also been applied to other groups in the past, such as youth workers, under Circular 4/88 (1988, since superseded): 'L.E.A.s should recognise the importance of maintaining the confidentiality between the young person and the youth and community worker as far as is consistent with safety' (Department of Education and Science, 1988).

While it may be argued that much of the above discussion focuses on and relates narrowly to sex education, the key issues of children's rights to autonomy remain absolutely central to the discussion. Therapeutic work in schools may be much broader than dealing with matters of sexuality, but these issues continue to be of crucial importance for many adolescents. The key issues for developing child-centred therapeutic practice in schools are, in fact, heavily bounded by the principles of choice and control fought over in the debate on sex education in schools – just as they were at the heart of the question of access to contraceptive advice decided by *Gillick*.

In summary, the context for therapists working in a school setting is one where the rights of adults appear to predominate over those of children. Under this 'welfare' approach, it is adults who decide what children need and how these needs are to be met – whether the need is for confidential counselling and therapy or for access to advice on sex, contraception and information about gay or lesbian sexuality. However, a space does exist for confidential therapy to be established. Independent legal opinion also endorses the role of professional judgement for teachers in providing information and counselling to pupils, despite the apparently prohibitive nature of successive circulars (Beloff and Mountfield, 1994). The possibilities for thus developing an explicitly child-centred form of therapeutic work are further explored in Part 2 of this book.

Participatory approach

Child care legislation from 1975 onwards has developed the principle that children have a right to take part in discussions about decisions affecting their lives. This has been endorsed by s. 22 of the Children Act 1989. It is also expressed by Article 12 of the United Nations Convention on the Rights of the Child 1989, ratified by the UK in 1991. The Convention recognises the need for 'the views of the child being given due weight in accordance with the age and maturity of the child'. This space for the child's active involvement in decision making has been noted earlier, with regard to issues concerning health care and divorce, in Chapter 1.

One expression of this participatory principle in the law is found in the right of children under 16 to initiate proceedings under s. 8, Children Act 1989 (Allen, 1992: 41–3). This concerns court orders 'giving directions for the purpose of determining a specific question which has arisen, or which may arise, in connection with any aspect of parental responsibility for a child'. They may take the form of a 'specific issue order' or a 'prohibited steps' order. Arguably, a child could apply for a specific issue order to obtain therapy which a parent, or figure with parental responsibility, was preventing them from receiving. Alternatively, a prohibited steps order might be obtained by such a parental figure to prevent a child seeing a therapist, however unlikely this may appear to be.

Children under 16 can apply for a s. 8 Order, but must first obtain leave of the court. This is only granted where the court 'is satisfied that he has sufficient understanding to make the proposed application' (s. 10(8)). Apparently fearing a flood of such applications, a Practice Direction was made in 1993 transferring applications by children from the lower levels of the court system to the High Court (Lyon and Parton, 1995: 49).

This 'participatory' perspective gives therapists more opportunity to place greater weight on the therapeutic relationship with the child, as distinct from subjecting it to the sometimes conflicting interests of third parties, such as parents or other authorities such as schools. There may still be some instances when the therapist may wish to override the child's wishes. This participatory approach to children's rights within counselling situations does not mean that the child's wishes will win out in every case. It simply requires that their wishes and views must be properly heard and acknowledged. In ethical terms, the therapist would perhaps be seeking to achieve a balance between promoting the child's autonomy and other competing interests, such as beneficence, non-maleficence and self-interest. The child's right to express an opinion and to have their feelings acknowledged is respected under this approach. However, other factors – such as their safety, their longer-term well-being or the interests of other parties, such as parents or other members of the family – may mean that another course of action is ultimately chosen, despite the child's stated wishes.

Independence model

A great deal of confusion and misinformation surrounds the third possible approach to therapeutic work with children. Based on the *Gillick* case, children under the age of 16 can be provided with confidential medical treatment, without first obtaining parental knowledge or consent, providing the doctor decides that the child is of 'mature understanding'. According to Lord Scarman, 'parental right yields to the child's right to make his own decisions when he reaches a sufficient understanding and intelligence to be capable of making up his own mind on the matter requiring decision' (*Gillick* v. *West Norfolk AHA* [1985] at 423). The Children's Legal Centre have deduced from this that 'mature children have the right to seek independent advice and counselling' (Children's Legal Centre, 1989b: 12). Based on this perspective, organisations such as Childline seek to provide confidential counselling to the child as the client, without first requiring parental consent.

The *Gillick* principle is shown in action in a court case to decide on the future care of an 11-year-old girl (*Re S, Guardian Law Report*, 1994). A court case was brought by her father to return her to his care in France after she had been illegally brought to the UK by her mother. The mother had acted wrongfully in so doing, breaking the terms of a previous court order in France concerning custody and contact provisions following the parents' legal separation. The Court of Appeal decided that it was entitled to take account of the child's wishes and feelings, if the child (named only as 'S') had reached an age and degree of maturity where it was appropriate to consider her views. The mother was legally bound to return the child to her father's care by the terms of the original court agreement made in France. However, the child definitely did not wish to return:

> the mother said that S did not wish to return to France. There was no independent evidence of S's views. The judge decided that it would not be appropriate for him to see S, but he asked the court welfare officer to interview S. The court welfare officer did so and gave evidence that S was 'very fluent and sophisticated' and that S wanted the judge told 'really, really strongly that she does not want to go back to France . . . because she feels great in England . . . she felt awkward and like a fish out of water at a French school . . . being forced to speak French . . . brought on her stammer which made her feel bad.' (*Guardian Law Report*, 22 July 1994)

Mr Justice Ewbank held that S had 'a "mature and rational view . . . based on genuine and cogent reasons"' (*Re S, Guardian Law Report*, 22 July 1994).

The process illustrates the weight given to the views of a girl judged to be of 'mature understanding' within the legal process. The example also gives a flavour of how her wishes were seen to be worth consideration, in that they were clearly and appropriately expressed, with convincing and credible reasons given for the feelings and views held. Her opinion was a deciding factor in the court's decision to permit her to stay in the UK.

From a therapeutic point of view, the *Gillick* principle provides the legal justification for working with the child as client, where certain conditions are clearly met. These factors include:

- The age of the child
- The degree of 'mature understanding' shown by the child
- The child's refusal to allow those holding parental responsibility to be informed
- The provision of advice or counselling being consistent with the child's best interests

In addition, there are certain immediate situations which may justify treating the child as being capable of making his or her own decisions. These include:

- Emergency
- Parental neglect
- Abandonment of the child
- Inability to find the parent

Clearly, judging the degree of 'mature understanding' of the child is both a crucial and a problematic issue for the therapist (Jenkins, 1997a). The central concept of mature understanding is essentially related to the child's competency to give valid informed consent to treatment or therapy.

The British Medical Association define competency in this context as: 'the patient's ability to understand the choices and their consequences, including the nature, purpose and possible risk of any treatment (or non-treatment)' (British Medical Association et al., 1993: 3). Translated into therapeutic terms, this would require the child to be able to understand something of what was involved in therapeutic work, and to be able to foresee the consequences, for themselves and for others, such as parents, in taking part in this relationship (Pearce, 1994). This would seem to require some degree of abstract conceptual thinking, along Piaget's model, of evaluating hypothetical alternatives. It would also require a move away, on the child's part, from strictly egocentric thinking patterns, to be able to grasp the possible effects of the child's choice upon significant others. This shift would be consistent with what Coles has described as a developing facility for 'moral intelligence' on the part of the child (1998).

Guidelines from the Children's Legal Centre (CLC) suggest a note of caution regarding the use of the *Gillick* principle in providing confidential counselling or therapy to children under the age of 16. The application of *Gillick* depends upon a case by case assessment of each child's degree of maturity and of their specific personal circumstances. Thus, adopting a blanket '*Gillick* policy' of guaranteeing complete confidentiality to all pupils in a given secondary school would thus 'not be good practice and would not stand if tested before a legal tribunal' (Children's Legal Centre, 1997: 3). Furthermore, the CLC point to the relevance of the child's age in determining maturity:

> While there is no legal decision which sets a minimum age at which children can be regarded as competent to consent to their own medical treatment, it is unlikely that many children under the age of 13 would be deemed competent to consent to medical treatment or counselling without the involvement of the parent. (1997: 3)

The example given above of the 11-year-old girl 'S' in the court case, while illustrative, should not be taken as evidence of some sort of a baseline in terms of the age for applying *Gillick*.

Recent dramatic case law, such as *Re R* [1991] and *Re W* [1992]), may appear to have undermined the legal protection of *Gillick* for therapists working with the child as client (see Chapter 8). However, these cases primarily relate to extreme and even life-threatening circumstances. Such extreme situations have included the case of a young persons's refusal to take anti-psychotic medication (*Re R* [1991]) and a similar refusal to consent to urgently needed medical treatment for anorexia nervosa (*Re W* [1992]) (see also Frantz, 1997). Despite these contrary legal decisions, the key principles of *Gillick* arguably remain intact for therapists working with the vast majority of young people under the age of 16.

The *Gillick* approach, however, brings its own real ethical dilemmas for the therapist, for example in judging how old the child needs to be for the *Gillick* principle to apply, and in assessing the actual level of 'mature understanding' that the individual possesses. The therapist here has to balance the potential gains in promoting autonomy by working solely with the child as client against the possible disadvantages of seeking prior parental consent. For therapists, while there may be much more therapeutic value in working directly with the child, their own sense of professional vulnerability and their legitimate concern with self-interest may be greatly increased should something be seen to go wrong. These very real concerns are explored in greater detail, with reference to specific examples, in later chapters.

Settings for therapeutic work with children

The previous section explored the relationship of therapeutic confidentiality to alternative models of children's rights. It is suggested that the therapist's ethical stance on confidentiality will, to a large extent, reflect their own personal and professional commitment to one or other of these approaches. The space for therapeutic work with children is constrained by other factors, which may go beyond the therapist's individual stance on these matters. Confusingly, children's rights – and, as a result, their rights within a therapeutic relationship – vary significantly according to the actual setting in which the therapy is provided. The diagnostic labels used to describe children's behaviour and distress can also vary significantly from one setting to another (Malek, 1991, 1993). It is not unknown for therapists themselves to become unsure of their real responsibilities and the extent of their freedom to work with the child as client.

School setting

As discussed above, therapeutic work in a school setting is ultimately governed by the doctrine of *in loco parentis*, reflecting a 'welfare' or paternalist approach towards children's rights. To summarise briefly, the sweeping education reforms of the 1980s gave additional rights to parents as consumers of education (Jeffs, 1995). The participative principles of the Children Act 1989, which seek to involve children in discussion and decision making, are explicitly held to end at the school gates and not to apply within the school itself. In addition, the effect of former Conservative government policy regarding guidance and counselling on sex education, contraception, and on the discussion of sexual orientation, has been to highlight the legal vulnerability of teachers in an already emotive and difficult area. This may well have inhibited teachers and therapists, who may be unclear about their freedom to explore these issues with concerned pupils, while avoiding the risk of legal redress by aggrieved parents.

Against this backdrop, however, the case for developing a child-centred form of therapy in schools continues to be strongly made (Bovair and McLaughlin, 1994; Cowie and Pecherek, 1994; Hill, 1994; Whitney, 1994). The exploration of the legal issues involved in providing counselling and therapy services within a school setting points to the potential for protecting such a space under the umbrella of the *in loco parentis* principle (British Association for Counselling, 1998a; Casemore, 1995). While children's rights are constrained in overall terms within the school system, they have not been removed entirely; therapists may thus seek to work in applying the *Gillick* principle with children as clients, . . . if key criteria are carefully met (Children's Legal Centre, 1997). There is, according to independent legal opinion, no specific requirement in law for parents' prior permission to be obtained before a child makes confidential disclosures to a teacher (Beloff and Mountfield, 1994). While parents may be unhappy or critical of confidential therapeutic work being provided to their child without their knowledge or consent, their rights do not necessarily predominate over the child's entitlement to such a service. It would follow, therefore, that a school could offer confidential therapy to pupils, based on applying the *Gillick* test to each pupil on a case-by-case basis.

Statutory agency setting

Besides schools, much therapeutic work for children is provided by statutory agencies, such as social services departments, the National Health Service, and the youth service of local authorities. The legal responsibilities of statutory agencies regarding children are largely, though not entirely, determined by the Children Act 1989. There are different strands which run through the Act, reflecting all three suggested models of children's rights. Child protection is framed in terms of protecting children's welfare, on the basis of adult decision making. However, the limits of this approach have been noted in the influential *Cleveland Report*, where its author stated that 'there is a danger that in looking to the welfare of children believed to be victims of sexual abuse the children themselves may be overlooked. The child is a person and not an object of concern' (Butler-Sloss, 1988: 245).

The alleged shortcomings of previous social work practice, in over-looking the views of children themselves, have been addressed in the Children Act 1989 – parts of which follow a much more participatory approach. The principle here is that children have a right to a say concerning social work decisions made about them, for example under s. 22 of the Children Act 1989. This approach is also consistent with Article 12 of the UN Convention on the Rights of the Child, to which the UK is a signatory.

Evidence of a more participatory approach to children can also be seen in the work of the courts, in relation to deciding on custody and contact in divorce or separation of parents, in adoption procedures and in the requirement to follow the 'welfare checklist' concerning exploration of the child's wishes and feelings before making orders in civil proceedings. Where the child is too young to take a meaningful part directly in proceedings, provision is made for their views to be obtained or expressed on their behalf by an advocate, such as a *guardian ad litem*, or court welfare officer. Given the imbalance of power to be found even in the most progressive of courts or case conferences, there is increasing scope here for the use of advocacy schemes such as those operated by groups such as the National Youth Advocacy Service (NYAS). In complex court cases, where children seek to contest court decisions up to the highest level, then the role of the Official Solicitor may be to pursue their case on their behalf as an advocate, even to the point of taking their case to the European Court of Human Rights at Strasbourg. In countries such as Norway, the role of children's advocates in society as a whole has been taken up with the official appointment of an Ombudsman for Children (Flekkoy, 1991).

The participative principles embodied in the Children Act 1989 are primarily to be found under s. 22 of the Act. This requires the local authority to ascertain the wishes and feelings of the child, 'so far as is reasonably practicable', when considering looking after them by providing accommodation. With regard to children legally in the care of the local authority, there is a wider duty:

> In making any such decision a local authority shall give due consideration –
> (a) having regard to his age and understanding to such wishes and feelings of the child as they have been able to ascertain . . .
> (c) to the child's religious persuasion, racial origin and cultural and linguistic background. (Children Act 1989, s. 22)

Again, a child in local authority care who is seen to have sufficient understanding may object to the appointment of a 'visitor' by the local authority, under s. 17 of the Children Act 1989.

The value of access to counselling and therapy is recognised by the legislation in a number of ways. The Children Act 1989 makes specific reference to the provision of counselling, primarily through Family Centres (Jenkins, 1993b). Also, the Guidance accompanying the Children Act 1989 acknowledges the need of children and young people in care for counselling and therapy which takes account of the particular concerns of black, gay and disabled children (Department of Health, 1991b: para. 9.50).

The status of the Children Act 1989 as a key reference point in the law about children can, however, be somewhat misleading for therapists. The Act brought together child care legislation in the form of public law, which regulates the activities of public bodies such as local authorities and health authorities, and private law. The latter concerns the resolution of legal processes concerning private individuals, such as divorce, contact, and parental responsibility by family members. In terms of public law, the Act is primarily addressed to the corporate responsibilities of the local authority as a whole, for example, in ascribing a duty to discourage offending, or to provide services to children with a disability. The local authority's duty to safeguard and promote the welfare of children is targeted at 'children in need', rather than at all children as such. Children in need are closely defined according to criteria relating to disadvantage or disability. The participative principles described above are linked to children who are in residential accommodation, hence 'accommodated' by the local authority, or who are formally in local authority care.

Unless therapists are working within this framework for the local authority or for a relevant voluntary organisation, then the participative principles of the Children Act 1989 may well not directly affect their therapeutic work with children. The child protection responsibilities of the local authority are heavily framed by the Act, with the duty to investigate suspected child abuse under s. 47. The relevance of the Act to therapists, in terms of imposing a duty to report such abuse, is much more equivocal unless they are directly bound by the child protection guidelines operated under their local Area Child Protection Committee. (This is discussed in more detail in Chapters 6 and 7.) In terms of the impact of private law, the potential impact of the Children Act 1989 for therapists may be slightly greater. Children may seek leave of the court, for example, to apply for a s. 8 Order, as outlined earlier. This may relate to an order seeking to obtain therapy against the wishes of a figure holding parental responsibility or to an action by such a figure to prevent the child continuing to receive such therapy.

Under the independence model of children's rights advanced above, there is an emphasis on the individual rights of the child under law. This is influenced by the *Gillick* ruling, which has opened the door to confidential medical treatment of children under the age of 16 who are seen to be of 'mature understanding'. This has had a major impact on counselling young people on matters of sexual health and contraception.

There is a wide range of rights to independent choice held by young people in particular situations (Fortin, 1999). Following the recommendations of the *Cleveland Report*, a child's consent is required for carrying out a medical or psychiatric examination made under an Emergency Protection Order (s. 44, Children Act 1989). Children are assumed to be a competent witness in criminal proceedings, under s. 52 of the Criminal Justice Act 1991. Likewise, in civil proceedings a child can give unsworn evidence if the court decides that he or she can speak the truth and has sufficient understanding to justify the evidence being given. Children may seek leave of the court to initiate certain proceedings under the Children Act 1989 and, if competent, can instruct a solicitor to act on their behalf (Houghton-James, 1994). Children also possess a qualified right to information via the Data Protection Act 1998, and may apply for access to health, education and social work records following the case brought by Graham Gaskin in the European Court (Gomien, 1991; Jenkins, 1997a). Children also hold the right to obtain compensation for abuse and criminal injury, for example, as a result of sexual or physical abuse. Children in care have a right to bring a complaint against the social services department, under s. 26, Children Act 1989. Children, finally, hold the right to sue via a private legal action, brought under the auspices of a 'next friend', such as a parent.

These rights within society as a whole do not always have an immediate relevance for therapists working with children, but rather form part of the wider context within which therapists may be working.

Voluntary agencies

Given the constraints affecting statutory bodies in terms of severely limited resources for therapeutic work, and the heavy onus on social services to operate complex and time-consuming child protection procedures, some of the greatest opportunities for child-centred therapeutic practice are to be found in the voluntary sector. Some voluntary child care organisations will operate policies regarding the provision of confidential therapy which closely parallel those of the statutory agencies. They may be party to specific policies on the reporting of suspected child abuse. However, other voluntary agencies, such as Childline, have developed ways of working which fit more closely the independence model derived from *Gillick* (Rayment, 1996).

Childline, a confidential telephone helpline and counselling service for children, was set up in 1986 following a huge public response to a BBC television programme on the topic of physical and sexual abuse of children. In 1995–96, Childline provided a counselling response for 90,000 children, nearly four times as many as when it first started ten years earlier. The calls cover a wide range of issues, including unhappy family relationships, problems with friends, and physical and sexual abuse. The number of calls received concerning bullying has increased by 14 times over the ten-year period, perhaps resulting from recent high profile media campaigns on this topic (Office for National Statistics, 1997: 151). The gender imbalance among callers is striking, with a ratio of four girls making calls for each boy. Childline's policy regarding confidentiality is to offer qualified, rather than completely unrestricted, confidentiality. The child's material is kept confidential unless 'the child is recognised to be in a situation that would lead to the child being in imminent danger of injury or death or a danger to themselves' (Children's Legal Centre, 1989b: 19). In one situation, where a child had taken an overdose before phoning Childline, the counsellor kept the child talking on the phone while the latter was slipping in and out of consciousness. Learning the name of the child's school, the headteacher was successfully traced and the child's address obtained from the school records. While the child was still talking on the phone, an ambulance arrived (Crompton, 1992: 208).

Within the limits of a service based on telephone counselling, Childline operates a policy of respecting children's rights as clients. According to the agency's Director of Counselling, 'children remain in control of what they say and what choices they make when they phone Childline and, as a result, they have been able to speak to us about their experiences without fear of rejection or unwanted intervention' (Harrison, 1994: 171). Where the child agrees, a referral to social services or the police will be made.

Private practice

The final setting to be considered is that of private practice. A therapist in private practice is not necessarily bound by the same legal concerns and duties as statutory agencies, such as those relating to child protection. There is no legal requirement on the private practitioner, for example, to report all suspected child abuse to the authorities, although the therapist would be justified in doing so in the 'public interest'. With regard to confidential therapy for children, the therapist in private practice enjoys a far higher degree of autonomy than professional colleagues who may be bound by contracts of employment, agency policies, or specific legal requirements related to their therapeutic work. The private therapist could work directly with the child as client; this does, however, beg the question of payment for the therapeutic work. The most likely scenario would be where parents agree to therapeutic work being carried out with their child, but agree to a negotiated contract where the therapeutic material remains confidential. Maintaining or breaching this agreement for confidentiality would then be at the discretion of the therapist.

Summary

Therapy with children is influenced, consciously or unconsciously, by a commitment to one of the three main approaches to children's rights. The welfare model prioritises the decision-making powers of adults who are responsible for children in their care, as under the *in loco parentis* principle in school settings. The participative model creates a space for children to have their views expressed and heard within the decision-making process, as in the case of some court hearings and in many social work procedures. The independence model places a high value on the autonomous choices to be made by the child, illustrated by the work of some voluntary organisations such as Childline and by the professional freedom available to therapists working in private practice. The actual dilemmas facing therapists seeking to work with the child as the client in the real world are both acute and complex. They are explored in more detail in Part 2.

Part 2   CASE EXAMPLES

5

Parental oversight of therapy: the therapist as mediator

Case study: Ellen

Ellen, a lively 12-year-old white, English girl, who was presenting increasingly disruptive behaviour throughout the school, referred herself for counselling. Ellen lived with her father and stepmother. From the initial session, Ellen insisted that her stepmother should not be informed about the counselling sessions. Ellen's reason for this was that she was afraid that her stepmother would prevent her from attending future sessions. This view was upheld and Ellen soon became positively engaged in the treatment process. Slowly her disruptive outbursts became less frequent. In spite of the positive results that were being achieved through the sessions, Ellen's disclosures were cause for considerable concern, as she outlined the level of neglect and physical abuse that she was experiencing. Her father did not arrive home from work until late in the evening; this meant that from the time Ellen arrived home from school, she was in the sole care of her stepmother. The usual pattern of events each evening involved Ellen receiving a small amount of food, then being locked in her room until the following morning. During one session, Ellen revealed a wound on her head where her stepmother had hit her, turning the ring on her hand around so that the sharp side would inflict the greatest damage during the blow. Ellen's disclosures in counselling were in turn reported to the social services department. The key social worker allocated to the case found it difficult to engage with the stepmother who was wary of all professionals. The latter clearly stated that she felt that 'all problems should be dealt with within the family and not through strangers'. Moreover, the girl's stepmother contacted the principal of the school and demanded that all counselling appointments should be ended immediately. Ellen protested and insisted that her appointments should continue; the principal, therefore, contacted the Local Education Authority to enquire into the legal position. The authority outlined their position, stating that parents were only legally bound to have their children attend lessons during school hours, and as there was no other legal obligation, the counselling would have to be ended. Following this, Ellen engaged in a bout of seriously disruptive behaviour and eventually made a physical attack on the principal. Soon afterwards, Ellen was sent to a special centre for disruptive pupils.

Legal and practice perspectives

The model of therapy being used here is one based on acknowledging the (assumed) right of a parent or other adult figure to have 'oversight' of the therapeutic process (see Chapter 3). This is distinct from a situation where the therapist is seeking to do therapeutic work with the family as a whole. For many therapists, their working situation is such that a degree of parental oversight or involvement is inevitable. In many statutory agencies, the process of referral and gaining access to a therapeutic service necessarily involves the parents in some way. In other settings, such as youth clubs, schools and voluntary agencies working directly with young people, then parental knowledge of the counselling or therapy may not be automatic.

In trying to work therapeutically with the child or young person, the therapist immediately faces a contradiction. On the one hand, they need to establish an atmosphere of trust and rapport: 'it is incumbent on the therapist to facilitate the provision of an environment in which the child is permitted free expression' (Harper, 1994: 167). On the other hand, however, the involvement or knowledge of parents or other authority figures may well inhibit and undermine this vital rapport. The result of this tension between the therapeutic needs of the child and the assumed right of the parents may result in a compromise agreement, whereby a triangular relationship of child, parents and therapist is created.

> As a very minimum a 'working alliance' between therapist and client has to be forged. In the case of children and adolescents, this contractual agreement to embark on a course of therapy frequently involves a 'three-cornered' commitment to the therapeutic endeavour. The literal dependence of children on their caretakers is an important consideration in treatment planning, and regarding 'customership' as being located in those persons who separately or jointly have the authority, the need and the means is an important consideration in therapy with children and young people. (Harper, 1994: 167)

Parental oversight of the therapy can take a number of different forms. It could involve a requirement for prior parental consent, an agreement to sharing either outline or more detailed information with the parents, and ultimately, parental control or veto, affecting the frequency and termination of therapy. The need to gain parental consent is stressed by some counselling services in schools: 'Parents are always consulted about a referral to the counsellor and their consent is necessary before counselling can proceed.' (Leaflet, Counselling Service, Dudley Metropolitan Borough Education Services). To summarise, this oversight of therapy may involve the parent or adult parental figure in terms of:

- Consent for the therapy to begin
- Knowledge in outline of therapeutic content
- Detailed knowledge of therapeutic content
- Control over frequency and termination of therapy

Working within this approach does not necessarily entail the therapist in an inevitable progression from seeking parental consent to making increasingly detailed disclosures about the content or progress of the work. Dudley's Education Department Counselling Service, referred to above, make this clear in a policy statement:

> Para. 2.1: The counsellors within the service have the right to exercise profes-
> sional judgement and discretion in withholding, temporarily or permanently,
> confidential information from the Headteacher, if by not doing so, the
> counselling relationship would be rendered inoperable.

While this policy is clearly spelled out with regard to the boundaries applying to parental oversight, in other cases it may be that adopting this approach leads to the gradual encroachment by the parent or other significant adult on the confidential work of the therapist and child.

Adopting a parental oversight model also brings additional figures into the overall framework, if not actually into the therapeutic relationship itself. In the case of Ellen, the headteacher, and later the social worker, also began to figure in the equation, with increasingly complex dynamics between all parties as a result (see Figure 5.1).

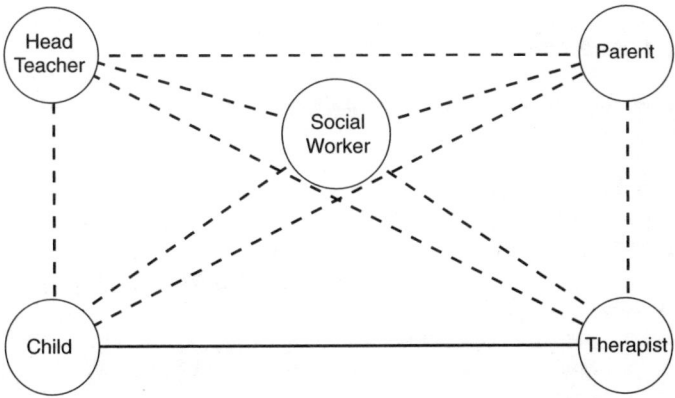

Figure 5.1 *The therapist as mediator: impact of external relationships on the therapeutic alliance*

The therapist may have assumed that the parent, or here the stepparent, had the right to veto further counselling sessions. However, as outlined in Chapter 1, parental rights have, historically, been in decline over the last two decades in English law. Lord Denning spoke of the parental right as 'a dwindling right' (*Hewer* v. *Bryant* [1970]). More recently, Lord Scarman stated that 'parental rights are derived from parental duty and exist only so long as they are needed for the protection of the person and property of the child' (*Gillick* v. *West Norfolk AHA* [1986]). Decisively, under the Children Act 1989, the concept of parental rights has been displaced by the term 'parental responsibility', meaning 'the responsibility for caring and raising the child to a properly developed adult both physically and morally' (*Hansard*, 1989). Section 3 of the Children Act 1989 defines parental responsibility as meaning: 'all the rights, duties, powers, responsibilities and authority which by law a parent of a child has in relation to the child and his property'.

In the situation described in this case study, the crucial question is whether the parent has the right to require prior permission concerning, or even to veto, confidential counselling at school. (In this situation, the stepparent, in effect, can be assumed to hold parental responsibility.) According to the legal opinion obtained from the Association of Teachers and Lecturers, parents do not have this automatic right (Beloff and Mountfield, 1994). While, in Ellen's situation, disclosure of physical harm had led to the involvement of social services, the counselling could have continued if authorised by the headteacher. Ellen's stepmother may well have felt aggrieved at such a decision, but her rights in law to prevent the continuation of the therapy are actually quite limited.

Rights of parents in school settings

The rights in law of parents, in school settings, are summarised below; they are the right to:

- withdraw their child from religious worship or religious education;
- receive information about the content of school sex education programmes;
- withdraw their child from sex education sessions (apart from the National Curriculum);
- opt out of medical and dental examinations of their child at school;
- make a complaint about the school's discharge of its responsibilities regarding the curriculum;
- receive reports on the child's progress at school;

- be consulted in the making of an Education Supervision Order for their child;
- appeal against a decision by the headteacher to exclude their child permanently from school;
- be informed about and vote in a secret ballot on changes in the school's grant-maintained status.

This may be a somewhat eclectic list, but note that it does not include an automatic right of the parent to be informed of confidential discussions that their child may have with a teacher or therapist employed by the school. The concept of parental rights, linked to the concept of the school acting *in loco parentis*, might combine and appear to mean that Ellen's stepmother had the automatic right of prior consent or ultimate veto of the therapy. This is, however, to misread the situation. The headteacher and the school authorities owe a 'duty of care' to their pupils. This is true of other professionals such as doctors, social workers and therapists, who owe a duty to their patients and clients. The concept of *in loco parentis* does not refer to the *content* of the duty of care, which would suggest an automatic compliance with parental wishes, but actually defines the *standard of care* that has to be met. The standard of care required of a teacher is to take such care as would be taken by a parent (Ramsay, 1992). This does not necessarily restrict or veto the child's right to confidentiality with a teacher, school nurse or therapist. The wide sweep of the changing law regarding children's welfare has increasingly moved away from an automatic stance of subordinating the child's wishes to those of the parent (Friel, 1998a). This can be seen, for example, in the broad development of the law regarding contact and residence in family proceedings, and with regard to medical treatment (see Chapter 1).

For Ellen's stepmother, grounds for bringing a private case under tort law against the school would be difficult to justify, as it would be hard to show what damage had been caused to her by the therapy taking place. Earlier cases have failed to establish that there is a tort of interference with parental rights as such (*F* v. *Wirrall* MBC [1991]). This case confirmed the position of the law after *Gillick*, namely that 'parental right . . . stems from the parental duty towards the child to care for and protect the child and is subservient to the welfare of the child' (Purchas LJ at 1151, *F* v. *Wirrall* MBC [1991]). Ellen's stepmother could not stop the therapy simply because she disapproved of it, or because it somehow detracted from her rights as a parent. She would need to show in some way that it was not furthering the child's welfare, which would clearly be a much more debatable issue.

One option might be for Ellen's stepmother to make a case that the school's policy conflicted with her rights as parent under the European Convention on Human Rights. The Convention is likely to be increasingly important as a reference point in the law in England and Wales, arising from its incorporation into the Human Rights Act 1998. The Convention has been the basis for successful cases in the past brought by parents against social services departments for excluding them from the process of making decisions about their children in care (*R. v. UK* [1988]; Gomien, 1991: 66). Under Article 8: 'everyone has the right to respect for his private and family life, his home and his correspondence'. The Convention goes on to state that there shall be no interference with this right by a public authority, with numerous exceptions, the most relevant one here being 'the protection of the rights and freedoms of others'. The right to family privacy is not, therefore, an absolute right. A court would have to balance the family's right to privacy against the possibly conflicting right of the child, under *Gillick*, to receive confidential therapy in order to promote their best interests.

In view of this, it may be that the education authorities were far too quick to comply with Ellen's stepmother's demands that the therapy end. In the absence of clear legislation or case law, there may still be the assumption that parental rights hold more force regarding school issues than they actually do in law. While schools will genuinely want to work in partnership rather than in opposition to parents, this should not be at the expense of the quite separate needs and rights of children. In child protection issues, the separation of the interests of child and parent has been established for some time, via statute and abuse investigation procedures (see Chapters 6 and 7). In the absence of such clarity regarding the issues around the school's meeting of the child's emotional needs, the danger is of capitulating to a notion of parental authority which is increasingly at odds with the developing law on this issue.

At best, Ellen's stepmother could make a complaint about the school's policy under s. 23 of the Education Reform Act 1988. Another option would be for her to seek a 'prohibited steps order' under s. 8 of the Children Act 1989, which would place the whole matter in front of the Family Proceedings Court but would not necessarily lead to the desired outcome from her perspective. The parent's rights are not as powerful here as might be assumed by the therapist or school authorities.

The child's rights are all too easily overlooked here. Arguably, Ellen has a strong moral and ethical right of access to therapy. (If denied help from the statutory or school setting, then she could still try to gain access to therapy via an organisation such as Childline.) Ellen has the right to give her informed consent under the *Gillick* principle, if the therapist were to judge her to be of 'mature understanding' and if her welfare required it, despite a refusal to permit her parents to be informed. Ultimately, she could also seek leave of the court herself, for a s. 8 'specific issue' Order, to enable the therapy to continue; but again, this may not be likely in the circumstances.

RIGHTS OF THE CHILD IN SCHOOL SETTINGS

Children within the school setting have the right to:

- give or refuse informed consent to medical treatment from age 16 (this may be overridden by the courts);
- give informed consent to medical treatment under 16, if of 'mature understanding' via *Gillick* test;
- have qualified access to their own school file if over 16;
- have their views and feelings considered in making an Education Supervision Order;
- express their views in any assessment regarding special educational needs.

This list provides a balance to the rights of parents – both actual and assumed.

Legal and practice perspectives – a summary

The headteacher owes an overall duty of care towards pupils, but this is somewhat narrowly interpreted by the law as being to act as 'a careful father' (*Williams* v. *Eady* (1893)) or as 'a reasonable, careful and solicitous parent' (*Rich* v. *London CC* [1953]). In reality, this is a somewhat limited standard to have to meet, compared with that of other professional groups. It is hard to see how permitting the therapy to continue against the parent's wishes would breach this duty, given that 'virtually all cases involving the liability of teachers and school authorities involve physical injuries sustained by students' (Ramsay, 1992: 9).

The therapist acted with the intention of protecting the child, by informing social services of the injury Ellen had incurred. (The issues involved in child protection are complex, and are explored in more detail in Chapters 6 and 7.) The therapist assumed in this case that reporting abuse was an obligation under a contract of employment, or under child protection guidelines – or under a general duty somehow applying to all citizens. While the legal issues relating to the parent's oversight of the therapy are complex, the therapist's reaction was the result of a lack of knowledge of the law and a consequence of a lack of access to informed and accurate legal advice. It is only on the basis of a clear understanding of the ethical issues involved, of the rights of the various parties concerned, and of the range of legal options available to the client, parent and relevant authorities, that the therapist can hope to act effectively in the client's best interest. Here, there is a case to be made that the continuation of therapy was in Ellen's best interests, and that the right of the child need not automatically be overridden, however forceful the demands of the parent.

Therapeutic perspectives

The initial point to consider is that of working with parental interventions. In order to avoid the kind of conflict with parents cited in Ellen's case, it may be more helpful to engage parents at the beginning of the child's therapy in order to gain their consent and support. This is clearly an approach which has been adopted with some success at one West London school (see Chapter 3). However, this approach is not without risk, as parents are not always willing to give consent. This parental power of veto prevents some children from ever gaining access to therapeutic treatment. Ellen provided clear insight as to how her stepmother might respond to her counselling. In the event, this proved to be extremely accurate. The stepmother clearly harboured anxieties about her own parenting methods; such fears can often lead parents to prevent their children from engaging in therapy. In view of this, it is unlikely that her stepmother would have agreed to Ellen's counselling from the outset.

Difficulties are dramatically increased, however, in cases such as Ellen's, when a parent is not involved at the beginning of the child's treatment but later learns about this through social services' involvement or via some other source. It is not surprising that the parent's anger will surface in such situations, which could have a damaging effect on the child's therapy. Perhaps the best hope for reparation in such circumstances lies in building up some form of dialogue between the parent or parents and therapist or other professionals. In a school setting, the headteacher may often be the first point of contact for the parent who makes a complaint about the child's therapy. It is, therefore, important that the headteacher is informed in advance of what is taking place. When difficulties arise, it is far easier for the headteacher to support the therapist from an informed position. The headteacher involved in the case of Ellen was highly supportive of the therapist's role in the school. Having been informed of Ellen's situation, she gave every assistance in trying to maintain her therapy; she also made every attempt to negotiate with the stepmother and gain her support for the therapy to continue. An empathic headteacher in such situations can become a valuable mediator.

It is important that the professionals involved in meeting parents in these situations do not take up an accusatory stance, but rather enable the parent or parental figures to discuss their own anxieties and difficulties. Ellen's stepmother, for reasons of her own – perhaps associated with her own childhood experiences – was having difficulty in caring for a stepchild. She was clearly receiving little support from her husband, who worked long hours away from home. The key social worker provided an opportunity for Ellen's stepmother both to discuss some of these issues and to engage with the social worker in supporting Ellen's therapy. A meeting was also arranged between the stepmother and the therapist, in order to reduce any anxieties which she held about Ellen's therapy. However, the stepmother turned down these opportunities for dialogue, maintaining her stance that all professionals were not to be trusted and she preferred to discuss difficulties only within the family. While professional mediation in some circumstances may prove positive, the difficulties of working with parental interventions following disclosure of the child being in therapy should not be underestimated.

Breaking confidentiality: effects on the child

The impact of disclosure to parents and outside agencies can often be damaging to the therapeutic alliance. This can be particularly acute when the child client has initially been offered a promise of confidentiality, which is then broken. Feelings of betrayal may lead the child to end treatment; alternatively the child may continue in therapy but avoid making any further significant disclosures. In Ellen's case, the immediate effect was that the therapeutic relationship was brought to a sudden end, at the stepmother's insistence. While this is an extreme reaction, it is by no means unusual; it should be emphasised that the risk of losing the client following parental interventions of this kind is considerable. In this situation there was no opportunity for Ellen to express her response to the breach of confidentiality (which had inadvertently lost her the therapy sessions) within the therapeutic setting. It could be suggested that she fostered angry feelings towards the therapist, but as she was unable to voice them within the sessions, they became displaced. It is quite possible that the attack on the headteacher, on an unconscious level, was aimed at the therapist. The attack actually involved biting the principal's hand, which somewhat brings to mind the saying 'biting the hand that feeds you'. It could also be the case that she was really biting the counsellor's hand for providing a nurturing experience, with the headteacher simply acting as a proxy for the therapist.

Given the opportunity to continue in therapy, Ellen's angry feelings might have been interpreted through the transference and have been successfully worked through. In returning to the notion of the therapeutic framework (Langs, 1979, in Chapter 2), it is clear that breaks in the frame need not be damaging if they are recognised as such by the therapist and an attempt is made to rectify the situation. In this respect, Patrick Casement describes instances from his own clinical work in which he made an attempt to listen to the messages given to him by patients, whenever he had broken the framework. As he stated, listening to these messages 'leads me eventually towards the necessary work of putting things right' (1985: 71). However, both Langs and Casement cite breaks in the framework as instances in which fairly minor breaks take place. These may involve personal disclosures by the therapist, the therapist's late arrival to a session, or a change in the fee charged. Casement cites an example in which he reversed the role of carer in a session, by asking his patient for help in finding a good dentist for himself (1985: 61). Such breaches, which will cause harm to the client, nevertheless seem minimal compared to breaches in confidentiality when working with children of the kind referred to in Ellen's case. The consequences may entail loss of privacy for the child client, the unwanted involvement of parents and outside agencies, and the potential loss of access to the therapy itself. It is questionable whether such breaks, and the consequent loss of faith in the therapist, can ever be repaired within the therapeutic alliance. The risk involved in disclosing confidential client material and protecting the child must, therefore, be balanced against the negative effects on the therapeutic alliance – and the potential for losing the client. The cases of Natalie and Maria further illustrate this point (see Chapters 6 and 7).

The therapist as mediator

Child therapists who choose not to offer their clients confidential access to treatment, or who breach confidentiality in the treatment process, will invariably be required to engage in some form of mediation outside the counselling setting. This may involve:

- meeting with the child's parents to gain consent and support in allowing the child to commence treatment;
- attending network meetings and case conferences with social services and police child protection teams following disclosures of abuse;
- meeting with parents following disclosure to explain the child's involvement in therapy and to gain their approval for it continuing;
- disclosing confidential details of the child's treatment to the senior member of the employing organisation;
- attending court cases to appear as a witness, and discuss previously confidential client material, following reported cases of abuse;
- supporting the child in applying for an order under s. 8, Children Act 1989, to enable them to remain in therapy.

Therapists who work with children may feel that it is not an intrusion on their role to act as a mediator in any of the above situations, if this helps to protect the child. Their view may be that the protection of the child is the main consideration, and the process of therapy is of secondary importance. However, many therapists may see stepping out of role in this way as wholly inappropriate. It could be seen that mediation, by the very fact that it involves taking action in the child's external affairs, inevitably causes harm to the therapeutic relationship. Therapists who act outside the therapeutic setting risk losing their anonymity and neutrality, as outlined in Chapter 2. It may be impossible to retrieve this stance later on, once the therapist has been seen by the client as someone who engages in negotiations outside the therapy, in addition to the child knowing that the therapist has breached their confidentiality.

The impact on the therapeutic relationship may be no less destructive, even when the initial outcome of mediation appears to be positive. For instance, the therapist may mediate with the parents at the outset of the child's counselling to gain their consent and support. While this may be successful, the parents are, from that point on, involved in some way in the child's therapy. It may then be difficult for both the therapist and the child to resist further unwanted parental intrusions into the process. The parents may contact the therapist for progress reports on a regular basis, and may make enquiries about the sessions' content. Refusal to disclose such information could create conflict or arouse feelings of envy in the parents, which could then have an adverse effect on the support offered for the child's therapy. The child may also feel unsafe in disclosing information to a therapist who is seen to be in constant contact with the parents. Parents may also make demands upon the child to disclose information about their sessions. This pressure may lead the child to end the treatment. Similarly, the successful mediation obtained through a court order may nevertheless have a negative effect on the therapeutic alliance. Embarking upon a counselling process following court proceedings, probably in direct opposition to parental wishes, could well cause difficulties for both the therapist and the child as client. The child may experience considerable conflict within the home, on a daily basis, concerning their continued participation in therapy. Living with such conflict may prove to be so unbearable that it is the child, rather than the parents, who eventually decides to end the therapy.

Within the working relationship, the therapist may be perceived by the child as someone who has engaged in open conflict with their parents. In this, there is a loss of the therapist's neutrality and a distortion of the assumed role of counsellor as one whose aim is to resolve conflict. Practitioners may conclude, therefore, that the only way to avoid a breakdown in the therapeutic relationship is to refrain from adopting the role of mediator. In pursuing this, preference is given to strict adherence to the role of therapist – working only with the internal world of the client, within an established and secure therapeutic framework.

6

Reporting child abuse: the therapist as law enforcer

Case study: Natalie

Natalie, an unhappy 14-year-old of Afro-Caribbean origin, disclosed details through her counselling sessions of her role in the family. She described her position as that of 'a family slave', and outlined details of the numerous domestic duties she was expected to perform on a daily basis. These largely involved a great deal of caring for her younger siblings and numerous housekeeping chores. In addition, she was frequently physically abused, sometimes by her mother but most often by her father. The most brutal assault by father was carried out using an electrical cable. The therapist assumed that there was a procedure in force which required automatic reporting of these incidents to the social services department. A network meeting was held, to which a number of professionals were invited. These included several members of the social services team, senior staff members of the secondary school that Natalie attended, and members of a police child protection unit. Her mother and father were also invited to the meeting but, while the mother was present, her father refused to attend. Natalie's mother gave her commitment during the meeting to try to deal with Natalie in a different way but, as he was not present, her father's level of commitment could not be assessed. Following this meeting, where the decision was made not to place Natalie on the child protection register, there was little follow-up work with the family. The reason given by the key social worker was that, due to extreme workload pressure on the department and lack of resources, the policy was to focus, to a large extent, only on 'life and death issues' (sic). As a consequence of the disclosure of her ill-treatment, Natalie was blamed by her family for reporting family affairs to the counsellor and, moreover, for bringing the police and social services into their lives. In order to avoid further confrontation, it seemed that Natalie needed to assure her parents that it had not been her decision to involve these outside agencies. As proof of this, and no doubt because she was so angry with the results of the intervention, Natalie ended the counselling. It is not known whether the abuse stopped but, most certainly, Natalie did not receive any further therapeutic assistance.

Legal and practice perspectives

The therapist's response in this situation raises the spectre of the automatic reporting of child abuse to the authorities. In fact, the legal situation applying here is complex, even without introducing a legal obligation to report abuse. A proposal to introduce mandatory child abuse reporting was considered and rejected, as part of the overhaul of child care law made in the 1980s. It was argued that such a requirement might:

> be counter-productive and increase the risks to children overall, first by weakening the individual professional's sense of personal responsibility and secondly, in casting the shadow of near automatic reporting over their work, by raising barriers between clients and their professional adviser and even between professionals concerned in the same case. (Department of Health and Social Security, 1985: para. 12.4)

It may be useful here to refer to the US experience of automatic reporting of child abuse, under the 1974 Child Abuse Prevention and Treatment Act (P.L. 93–247). This substantially increased the range of people with a responsibility to report suspected child abuse, from doctors to all health professionals; it also extended the categories requiring a report, from physical abuse to include neglect, as well as emotional and sexual abuse. The Act has had a major impact on the volume of reporting, but a much more doubtful effect in terms of dealing effectively with child abuse as a social issue. In 1992, out of two million reports made to National Child Abuse and Neglect Data Systems, over half of all reports were estimated to be unfounded (Levine et al., 1995: viii). Furthermore, the increase in the number of reports made has not produced a proportionate increase in the number of positive findings of abuse, nor has it resulted in additional resources being made available to those being investigated (1995: 7).

Under the law in England and Wales, not only is there no automatic reporting under the Children Act 1989, as is sometimes wrongly assumed by therapists, but there is no duty on the individual citizen to report child abuse. According to Lord Justice Staughton, 'a private citizen . . . may see a child in need but pass by on the other side' (M v. *Newham LBC* [1994] at 581). Thus adults who witnessed the ill-treatment of James Bulger could not be held to be legally at fault for not intervening (Morrison, 1997). However, any citizen may take action such as reporting abuse to the authorities in the 'public interest', in order to prevent a serious crime. A therapist working with Natalie in private practice would, therefore, have had professional discretion in deciding whether or not to report abuse, just as would any citizen.

Child protection requirements

A therapist may not be under an obligation to report all suspected abuse, but there may be requirements deriving from their work for a particular agency or from statutory guidelines which would require them to do so. Many therapists assume that this is required under the Children Act 1989, when it is the guidelines under *Working Together* which probably have more relevance here (Home Office/Department of Health, 1991). Under s. 47 of the Children Act 1989, the local authority is required to investigate cases where it is suspected that a child in their area is suffering or is likely to suffer 'significant harm'. Certain agencies, such as the local education authority (LEA), and housing and health authority (HHA) are required to assist with these enquiries, 'in particular by providing relevant information and advice'. However, apart from those specified or authorised by the Secretary of State, this part of the Act 'does not oblige any person to assist a local authority where doing so would be unreasonable in all the circumstances of the case'. As stated previously, the Act is addressed to local authorities in outlining their duties with regard to children, particularly the group of children defined as being 'in need' according to disadvantage or disability criteria. Where a person is working for the local authority, it is likely that their contract or conditions of employment will require them, as a social worker or an advice worker, to pass on information about child abuse.

The actual mechanics of child protection are spelled out in the key policy document, *Working Together* (see Home Office/Department of Health, 1991). This sets out in detail the operation of child protection procedures, as part of the work of the Area Child Protection Committee (ACPC). This is a multi-disciplinary body bringing together representatives of social services, health, education, the police, and voluntary organisations – all charged to set down clear policies and guidelines for protecting children reported to be at risk of abuse. In part, this includes the operation of a system of registration of children onto the 'at risk' or child protection register, according to categories of neglect, physical, emotional or sexual abuse, where case conferences have recommended that a child should be registered.

Teaching staff are generally included under the remit of child protection guidelines devised by the ACPC. The duties of teachers covered by ACPC guidelines for reporting child abuse are also set out in detail in DfEE Circular 10/95:

> Staff have a professional responsibility to share relevant information about the protection of children with other professionals, particularly investigating agencies. If a child confides in a member of staff and requests that the information is kept secret, it is important that the member of staff tells the child sensitively that he or she has a responsibility to refer cases of alleged abuse to the appropriate agencies for the child's own sake. (Department for Education and Employment, 1995: para. 27)

This apparently binding duty on teachers has presented a dilemma for counsellors working in further education (FE) settings. Under procedures outlined in Circular 13/96, the Association of Colleges proposed that counsellors working in further education would be required to report all instances of child abuse within two hours (Association of Colleges, 1996). This mandatory duty to report all child abuse would place therapists working in colleges in a quandary regarding confidentiality. For example, in counselling a mature student for depression, the client may reveal having lost her temper and hit her teenage son for being 'out of order'. If the counsellor is under a blanket requirement to report all abuse, then doing so might jeopardise the therapeutic work being done with the mother; not to report might leave the son at risk of further physical harm. Failure to report abuse might also be seen as a breach of the employment contract or conditions of service by the college authorities.

The impact of this real dilemma, voiced by the Association for University and College Counselling led the British Association for Counselling to seek legal advice from John Friel, a barrister. This advice carries the limited status of a legal opinion, rather than the judgement of a court on the matter, but is nevertheless useful in clarifying some of the key issues here. The advice stressed the 'fiduciary duty' placed upon the therapist in such a situation to maintain the trust placed upon them by the client. This fiduciary duty may be expressed in terms of a clear contract, spelled out in a professional code of ethics, in order to protect confidentiality with the client.

> A contract which obliges disclosure in all cases where abuse is suspected or reported has in my view the effect of abrogating the duty of confidence. It effectively places the duty on the counsellor to disclose in all circumstances where some sort of abuse is reported, outside the law of confidentiality, without any consideration of their own professional judgement and duty . . . It would also be a breach of their fiduciary duty. (Friel, 1998b: para. 11; see also Bond, 1998)

Friel's opinion is valuable in reinforcing the notion of the therapist's professional discretion in reporting abuse, exercised while using supervision, and being guided by a well-considered code of ethics. However, actual case law on this point is rare, as with many points of law relating to therapists. While it may be that a court of law would support the stand taken by a therapist in not reporting child abuse, this course of action may still leave the individual practitioner open to disciplinary proceedings or even to dismissal by an unsympathetic employer. Referring to a professional code such as that of the BAC would clarify the thinking behind a therapist's decision to report or not to report abuse. Such a code has the limited status of a voluntary professional set of guidelines, as opposed to an enforceable statutory code such as the Mental Health Act Code of Practice or General Medical Council 'Blue Book', which accordingly carry greater authority in legal proceedings. However, as Bond argues:

> The critical issue is not the status of the BAC's Code, which merely restates the common law in general terms. The critical issue is whether or not a particular practitioner is subject to some statutory requirement or specific decision in case law requiring an obligation to report. A contractual or disciplinary term is unenforceable against a common law obligation of confidentiality. (Bond, 1999)

The stark ethical and legal conflict here is, therefore, between a therapist's contract of employment – perhaps requiring mandatory child abuse reporting – and their wider common law duty to maintain confidence with the client.

This emphasises the very real dilemmas facing therapists in reporting child abuse, where their contract of employment, local child protection guidelines and advice from their professional association's code of ethics may well not be in agreement. For the therapist working in a school setting, it underlines the necessity of setting out clear policy regarding confidentiality, endorsed by the headteacher, communicated to clients and staff, and held to by the individual therapist. The considerations affecting child abuse reporting by therapists may be summarised as follows:

- Nature of contract concerning confidentiality with client and agency
- Child protection guidelines relating to *Working Together*
- Contractual obligation to employer or agency
- Fiduciary duty of trust and confidentiality to client
- Public interest in reporting or preventing a serious crime
- Child's own wishes and feelings if of 'mature understanding', following the *Gillick* principle

Child protection procedures

In the particular situation in this case study, the therapist felt bound to comply with the existing child abuse reporting procedures. This then activated an investigation by the local authority child protection team, under s. 47 of the Children Act 1989, to assess whether the child was at risk of 'significant harm', either physical or emotional. Therapists, and clients themselves, often feel that they lose control to the dictates of an unfamiliar and powerful bureaucratic system by making such a report. Investigation of the referral by a social worker may result in a visit to the family to gain more information. Depending upon the outcome of this, a case conference of involved professionals, including representatives from education, may be convened to clarify the nature of the perceived risk to the child, to decide upon registration on the child protection register, and to decide on a plan of action – including allocating resources to meet the family's and the child's needs.

Teachers and staff from education have a major role to play in the reporting of suspected abuse; teachers, school nurses and Education Welfare Officers make 23 per cent of child protection referrals (Department of Health, 1995: 29). However, the role of education staff in the unfolding child protection process is much less clear.

> The role of teachers is particularly confused. They spend more time with children than any other professional group and education services refer the most cases to the child protection process. Nevertheless, other professionals remain unclear about the role of education in child protection and teachers remain unclear about their own contribution. (1995: 27)

The process of placing a child's name on the 'at risk' or child protection register may be seen as the end of the procedure but, in reality, it only marks a stage in the coordination of professional intervention in the family's life. There is wide variation between different local authorities in terms of their registration of children 'at risk'. This is due in part to socio-economic factors such as housing, poverty and deprivation, but also due to the differing ways in which registers are operated (Office for National Statistics, 1997: 150). Figure 6.1 provides an overview of the possible outcomes of referral and investigation for child abuse.

The crucial question is whether registration of the child as being 'at risk' actually brings about the provision of necessary resources, or results in real help for the child and family in question. In some cases, registration is the

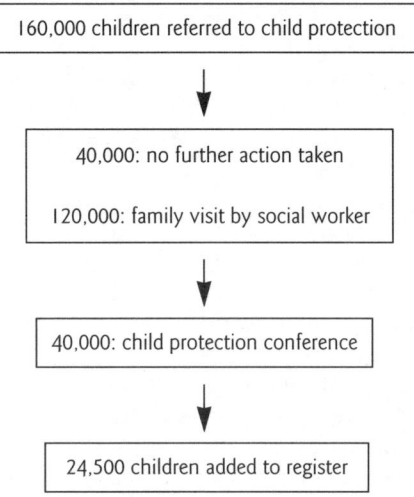

Figure 6.1 *Estimated annual outcomes of child protection investigations under Working Together*

Source: Department of Health, 1995: 28

trigger needed to produce the allocation of such resources, such as specialist help at a local authority or voluntary-run Family Centre. However, this is not always the case. Sometimes, the bruising process of the investigation by social services produces after-effects that mean any chance of cooperation from the family has been destroyed. Registration may not even mean that the case will be allocated to a social worker in extreme situations in some urban boroughs, where resources for follow-up work are inadequate. This has led to the criticism that the child protection framework in England and Wales is heavily skewed towards the investigation of abuse but away from provision of adequate resources for follow-up, including access to therapy for children and parents alike (Kennedy, 1997).

For a child such as Natalie, where the link between the therapist and child had been broken, the need for continuing therapy to be taken up by social services, or by another body such as the NSPCC, is urgent. Yet, in some cases, the resources for such therapeutic work are lacking. It may also be the case that social workers describe their work in therapeutic terms, when this is not strictly accurate, according to the Department of Health's own report, *Child Protection: Messages from Research*: 'what social workers provide is not treatment in a clinical sense. . . . The researchers consistently found that professionals confused therapy and support' (1995: 36).

The hostile response of Natalie's mother to social work investigation is not uncommon. It may have been that she and her partner would not have cooperated in any case, short of the threat or reality of actual court proceedings. In this situation, her refusal to work with the social services, and their lack of resources for follow-up work, meant that no further effective work could be done. The Guidance to the Children Act 1989 spells out a need for the principle of partnership to apply with working relationships between parents and professionals. The research suggests that necessary understanding between parents and professionals was most likely to occur if there was agreement about:

- 'whether the child had been abused
- who was responsible
- who was to blame
- whether the child was at future risk'. (Department of Health, 1995: 37)

In the absence of such agreement between Natalie's parents and the social services, further work to explore or remedy the family's difficulties was unlikely to succeed.

From the moment Natalie made her disclosures of ill-treatment to the therapist at school, she became a passive focus of the child protection procedure, with limited regard shown for her rights as a person within this process. The child's right to participate in child protection proceedings is spelled out under the Children Act 1989, both within social services' deliberations and within court proceedings (see Chapter 4). However, it is all too easy for the child's voice to be lost amidst the welter of activity by concerned professionals (Schofield and Thoburn, 1996).

Therapeutic perspectives

It is not known whether the act of automatic reporting actually produced any positive results in Natalie's home situation, as the social services were unable to maintain any monitoring procedures to ensure that the abuse had stopped. What is known is that for a time her relationship with her family worsened, in that she was constantly blamed for what they perceived as an unwanted intrusion by outside agencies into their lives. The pressure on Natalie in this regard led to the breakdown of the therapeutic process. This deprived her of the opportunity fully to explore her internal world and prevented any possibilities of her reaching a position of empowerment. Again, Natalie's situation is not uncommon and risks of this kind have to be considered when deciding whether to report child abuse.

The alternative to the automatic reporting of abuse in such instances could be perceived as involving some risk for the therapist concerned, given that the abuse might be continued or could become increasingly dangerous to the child. However, in the case of Natalie the social services did not assess her position to be life threatening. Indeed, Natalie was 14 years old and in her daily life came into contact with a number of adults outside the family, such as teachers, neighbours and members of the extended family. Had Natalie's situation become unbearable or life threatening, she could have undoubtedly sought their help – an option also open to children in similar cases, even if they are younger. Yet it would seem that in such cases therapists often develop a powerful omnipotent counter-transference, in which there is a belief that only they are able to rescue the child. Powerful feelings of anxiety also emerge in which terrible repercussions for not having protected the child are fantasised. All clients, and most particularly abused children, will project their anxieties onto their therapists. For successful therapy to take place, it is imperative that therapists should avoid acting upon such feelings. As child psychoanalyst Hannah Segal points out: 'it is the analyst's acceptance and understanding of these projections, without acting them out, and the gradual conveying back to the patient of the psychic content, that gives to the patient the basic security of being contained in the psycho-analytic situation' (1986: 120). It is worth considering that the decision to report instances of abuse may be largely influenced by the inability of the therapist to contain anxiety, rather than the actual degree of danger to the child (Copley and Forryan, 1997: 193–4).

Child protection and the child's right to therapy

While mandatory reporting is not compulsory for all therapists in England and Wales, many organisations will have a policy on child protection issues which will require professionals to report instances of abuse. Counsellors and therapists, however, may operate under a separate professional code of ethics which prioritises confidentiality and allows for professional discretion. It is, therefore, possible that in a school situation, for example, the teachers may be obliged to report suspected instances of abuse while the therapist may exercise a degree of professional discretion, operating under a separate code of ethics.

For potential clients, this clear difference distinguishes the therapist from the teacher. There is often general understanding among pupils that the counselling setting is private and confidential. There is also general acceptance that the practitioner will be able to offer specialist skills and techniques which other professionals do not have. In the case of Natalie, the teaching staff at the school were warm, caring and approachable. There were many opportunities for Natalie to discuss her home situation with a number of teachers, most particularly the form tutor amd the head of year teacher, who both held pastoral roles and readily made themselves available to their students. However, neither Natalie nor the other children cited in the case studies chose this option. All voiced their opinion, at some point, that they preferred to bring their difficulties to the confidential counselling setting. They stated that, although they liked certain teachers, they did not trust that if they disclosed information to them the material would remain confidential.

It cannot be assumed that in these and similar situations, the child client who makes risky disclosures within the therapeutic setting is simply asking for protection. If so, then it is wondered why they would elect to tell an adult who had made a pledge of confidentiality, rather than another adult who would readily act upon such information. It is possible that a child might not make a conscious decision to disclose such information at the outset of treatment, but that the therapeutic setting helps the child to discuss such issues, perhaps for the first time. In one such situation, a female client took six months to begin to talk to the therapist about instances of abuse in her early childhood. Soon after, she was able to talk openly about these experiences to her new local GP, after only two meetings with him. It seemed easier for this client to talk about her experiences once they had been verbalised for the first time. In the cases cited, however, it appeared to make no difference whether the disclosures came quite soon into the process or whether this took numerous sessions. What was significant is that in all cases there was no desire for the children concerned to repeat this information to any other adults, or to have the therapist repeat it. It seems that the children in these circumstances were actually seeking solutions to their difficulties solely through therapeutic intervention (Wattam, 1999).

However, ironically perhaps, therapists who seek solutions through setting child protection procedures in motion may deny children their right to therapy and an opportunity to explore their internal world. Children's rights are again overlooked in favour of child protection; it is the adults who make the decisions about which solutions are the most viable. The view often prevails that children do not have the maturity to make such decisions concerning their own therapy. Yet children who decide to embark on a therapeutic process have already made a mature decision about which approach they would like to take to resolve their difficulties, as is shown by the type of professional they have elected to speak to. They have also shown considerable maturity in seeking out that professional, often with far greater difficulties in gaining access to treatment than those encountered by adults.

Children are not in a position to pay for their treatment, which limits their choice regarding which therapist they see, when and where. They do not have the freedom of time and movement that adults have, and may have to go to great lengths if they wish to keep all knowledge of their therapy confidential. Careful planning and foresight are often demon-strated in arranging contact with a therapist. Many children, some of them quite young, organise their time and money in order to make telephone calls from public callboxes to contact telephone counselling agencies. Others arrange appointments at drop-in centres or ask school teaching staff to deliver notes requesting appointments to the counsellor. Appointment times are remembered and children frequently take sole responsibility for getting themselves to sessions. Once engaged in sessions, children often work through their difficulties with courage and tenacity, remaining in treatment for several years – sometimes without the support of parents or other adults.

These actions are mature and well thought out, and the children involved have elected to see a particular type of professional, in a specific setting. They are, in effect, making a very clear statement that they are not asking for protection through any form of action, but are in fact seeking an opportunity for confidential therapeutic treatment. If children are prepared to make such efforts to gain access to therapy, and are able to make use of the process with the same ability as adults, then it is highly questionable whether their right to therapy should be denied. Natalie is one of many children in similar situations denied the right to therapy, albeit inadvertently and with good intentions, by the only professionals who have the potential to offer such a service.

The therapist as law enforcer

For effective therapeutic work to take place, it is essential that clients are able to talk without restriction of any kind. It is accepted that the main contributing factor which enables this process of free association is the promise of confidentiality (see Chapter 2). Child therapists who offer a contract of confidentiality but then breach this because of risky disclosures are, in effect, 'policing' the child's thoughts. Some practitioners attempt to avoid what can be seen as a betrayal in this respect, by embarking on a different contract with child clients. In this, a general pledge of confidentiality is made from the beginning but with the added proviso that, should the child disclose anything which is a cause for concern, then this sensitive information may be taken to outside agencies. This would correspond to the concept of a contract of conditional or provisional confidentiality described in Chapter 5.

While this approach may reduce the therapist's anxiety, it may actually increase the anxiety of the child. In effect, the child's thoughts under this contract have been policed from the outset. The natural consequence under such a contract is for children to refrain from talking about what might be the most important issues in their lives. They may find the internal conflict of attending sessions, while holding back information, too difficult to endure and, therefore, leave the process. For some children such a contract is unclear and confusing; they may wonder exactly what information the therapist will contain and what will be disclosed. Such confusion will undoubtedly develop from the therapist's own confusion about which role is being performed at any given point in the process. The practitioner may perform the natural role of therapist, making well-timed interventions and interpretations in response to client material. Alternatively, the therapist may abandon this approach and step into the role of law enforcer, reporting client material to the police or the social services.

The role of therapist may have to alter considerably once reporting has taken place in instances of child protection. In the case of Natalie, the therapist soon became involved in attending a network meeting and in giving written evidence to a number of professionals, including the police, in a large social services conference room. In more serious cases, the therapist may be required to give evidence in the courtroom as a witness. These activities are far removed from that of interpreting the material of the child's inner psyche, on a one-to-one basis, in a private setting.

It is difficult to know why therapists wish to adopt the role of law enforcer when there are members of the police force available who have been specifically trained to deal sensitively with child protection issues. The therapist may perceive the child as being too young or too frightened to take the daunting step of walking into a police station and reporting abuse. Yet, if the child desires to make contact with the police, for their own protection, then there are alternative methods – and children have shown themselves more than equal to such a task.

It can be seen from the number of calls received by Childline each year that the telephone can be used competently and comfortably, even by younger children, when needed. It would be no more difficult for a child in danger to dial the well-known emergency number rather than that of Childline. Indeed, Childline will contact the police or social services on the child's behalf, if that is what the child is asking for (otherwise confidentiality is maintained). Alternatively, as stated above, there are many adults who children come into contact with on a daily basis, to whom the child could refer for support if they felt unable to make direct contact with the police. These options are not used by children such as Natalie because they do not want to inform the police of their situation. They, therefore, choose to disclose this information to the only adult who they perceive can be trusted to keep it confidential and who will deal with it in a way specific only to a therapeutic process.

The child may wish to use the therapeutic process to assist them in reaching a decision about whether they would like to take action about their situation. The practitioner who maintains the role of therapist will be in a position to enable the client to make such a decision and then continue to offer therapeutic treatment should the child decide to involve outside agencies. The therapist who takes on the role of the law enforcer, however, may confuse the client sufficiently for the child to lose faith in the therapist and/or to end treatment. As seen in the case of Natalie, the involvement of social services and police child protection teams with the family can create further difficulties for the child, who may suffer both guilt and persecution for 'causing' the intrusion. It is vital in these situations that there is therapeutic follow-up work. As illustrated in the case of Natalie, the therapist who has acted as law enforcer may no longer be seen by the child as the person most suitable to provide therapeutic treatment; the bond of trust has been broken.

7

Provisional confidentiality in practice: the therapist as protector

---

Case study: Maria

Maria was a timid but extremely articulate 12-year-old Greek Cypriot girl, who presented a complex chain of events throughout the two years that she was in treatment. After a number of sessions, Maria disclosed that her brother-in-law had been touching her in a sexual manner since the age of 11. As this situation was still continuing, the therapist made the decision to involve outside agencies in order to prevent further abuse. The client was most reluctant to consent to this proposal as she felt that she was somehow to blame, and would be blamed by her family for the abuse. Nevertheless, she conceded.

Maria's prediction that she would be blamed came to fruition. Contact was made with the family by an experienced and competent team of social workers. However, the social workers were not successful in enabling the family to take responsibility for protecting their child. The brother-in-law was a valued member of the family and was also a partner in his father-in-law's business. The police cautioned him, saying he was not to enter his in-laws' family home. Yet, as time passed, he increased the frequency of his visits. He moved from waiting outside in his car, to eventually using the house as his second home, as he had always done in the past. While the immediate abuse ceased, her brother-in-law's presence alone caused Maria considerable anxiety. It seemed that the anxiety was not totally related to the abuse, but rather because the family loyalty for the son-in-law created considerable tension during his visits. Follow-up work by social workers only seemed to worsen what had now become a volatile situation. After each of the visits by social services, life became increasingly difficult for Maria. Her father felt that his daughter had brought this upon herself, through her adoption of an attractive and fashionable Western code of dress. Her elder sister felt betrayed and gave every support to her husband, the alleged abuser. Maria's mother began to display symptoms in which it appeared she was experiencing a psychotic breakdown. Maria described situations in which she had witnessed her mother eating the contents of the rubbish bin and attempting to strangle herself with a curtain. It was Maria herself who eventually pleaded with social services not to visit the home anymore, in an attempt to avoid further disturbing and disruptive scenes.

Maria was left to deal with a most unsatisfactory situation in her everyday living environment. Previously, she had experienced considerable freedom. After her reporting of the abuse, her family prevented her from leaving the house. They all became highly critical of the way she dressed and styled her hair. There followed a great deal of conflict between herself and the family on a daily basis. Maria worked through some of these issues in her therapy sessions, which she continued to attend on a twice-weekly basis. Maria's commitment to the process was significant, given the breach in confidentiality that had taken place. Yet something had inevitably been lost in the therapeutic alliance and Maria began to take her difficulties to a male teacher in the school. The teacher took full advantage of the vulnerable then 14-year-old girl, whom he took into his confidence. It appeared that something was amiss when Maria disclosed that the teacher had given her presents. Following the summer holiday, she disclosed that he had looked up her home telephone number in the school records, contacted her and taken her out several times. Maria, though having been quite open during the two years of treatment, would not disclose whether she was having a sexual relationship with the teacher. When asked why she found this difficult to talk about, she replied, 'Whatever I tell you, I know you have a responsibility to inform social services. I might even have to go to court, and I know my family will blame me. . . . I'm not going through all that again.'

It seemed that Maria's statement gave a good indication that a sexual relationship was taking place, in which case the teacher was abusing his professional duty and breaking the law. It was felt that it was the therapist's ethical duty to attempt, at least, to have this teacher removed from the all girls school, if not disbarred entirely from the teaching profession. Yet this depended upon Maria making a definite statement, which would inevitably lead to a court case and possibly to abandonment by her family: the two things she feared most. Having once been quite open in sessions, Maria from then on began to discuss only superficial issues and feelings. She was clearly correct in sensing that the rule of total confidentiality was no longer in operation. With this, the therapeutic alliance disintegrated, and the remaining sessions were shallow and unproductive.

Legal and practice perspectives

In making the decision to report abuse, the therapist sets in motion a series of procedures which have as their focus:

- the investigation of the risk or harm affecting the child;
- protection of the child from further harm or abuse;
- provision of help and support to the child and family;
- possible legal action via civil proceedings and criminal prosecution.

This is a complex, interlocking set of procedures which is often seen as somewhat opaque by therapists who are not already familiar with health or social work practices. It can be even more frightening and overwhelming for the child or, alternatively, it can bring a sense of relief that something is now 'being done'. Even here, there may be acute conflict between the child's immediate wishes and the longer-term priorities of the child protection system and the legal system as a whole. The child may simply want the abuse to stop. The wider public interest may instead see the removal of the child from home as necessary, and the prosecution of the alleged abuser as desirable. Within this complex process, the child's wishes now come second to those of other, more powerful professional and judicial interests.

The child protection process can be seen as containing a curiously adult-centred logic:

> A self-confirming cycle is established. Children are perceived as lacking competence to take responsibility for their own lives and therefore as vulnerable and in need of protection. Because they need protection, adults are vested with powers to act on their behalf. Because children are denied the powers to make decisions or fully participate in them they are rendered more vulnerable to the authority of adults. (Lansdown, 1995: 34)

Outcomes of social services intervention

As outlined in Chapter 6, the reporting of abuse will normally trigger an investigation by the local authority social services department. The duty of the local authority is to investigate where a child is suffering or is likely to suffer 'significant harm' – a key phrase in the wording of the Children Act 1989.

In investigating the alleged abuse, the social services may contact other agencies for information, agencies such as the school, the health authority or relevant voluntary agencies, for example the National Society for the Prevention of Cruelty to Children (NSPCC). The child concerned may be interviewed and possibly offered a medical examination. A visit to the family may then be made, following which it may be decided to convene a case conference to pool information known about the child and family by concerned professionals. The focus of the case conference is to decide on the degree of risk to the child, to register the child on the child protection register if necessary, and to decide on any further action. Such action may include providing voluntary social work help to the family, perhaps via providing a place at a Family Centre or by offering residential accommodation for the child. The business of the case conference may also include making a decision about taking civil proceedings to ensure the welfare of the child or of other children in the family (see the summary of the main stages of child protection procedures below). The police child protection unit may also initiate a criminal prosecution of the child's alleged abuser. Each of these outcomes has a direct bearing on the child's situation

– and on the child's ability to participate in the decisions being made about their own future. The main stages of child protection procedures are listed in summary below.

1. Local authority duty to investigate where a child is suffering 'significant harm' under s. 47, Children Act 1989:

- contact with other agencies to gather information;
- investigative interview with child;
- possible medical examination of child;
- family visit to gain further information about alleged incident.

2. Case conference to share information provided by professionals and family members:

- decision on whether to place child's name on child protection register;
- future planning. Options include:

   - social work help, such as a place at a Family Centre or 'looking after' child in local authority accommodation;
   - civil proceedings, such as care proceedings;
   - criminal prosecution of alleged abuser;
   - decision to take no further action.

Source: Home Office/Department of Health, 1991, *Working Together*

In Maria's case, the decision of the case conference was to offer social work help to the family on a voluntary basis, rather than to take civil proceedings to ensure her safety through a court order. The voluntary social work support offered seemed to take account of her religion and ethnicity, at least to the extent that a male Greek Cypriot social worker was chosen to work with her and the family. The risk here is of adopting a stereotypical perception, either of her family as a 'closed system' or of Maria herself as a passive victim, at odds with restrictive cultural and family values (Jackson, 1996: 6). In fact, Maria was offered the possibility of being referred to a counsellor from her own culture, but she chose to remain with her original therapist.

The police decided to caution the brother-in-law, rather than to prosecute, possibly given the lack of substantive evidence of abuse. In other circumstances, the outcome may well have been different. Under the Children Act 1989, the courts have a wide range of options for deciding the welfare of the child. The child's welfare holds paramount importance for the court concerning any decisions made about the child's upbringing. The main options open to the courts are described in the summary of the Children Act 1989 below.

SUMMARY OF THE CHILDREN ACT 1989

Children at risk of harm can be protected in the short term by use of:

- s. 47: local authority duty to investigate children suffering 'significant harm'
- ss. 44 and 45: Emergency Protection Orders. The local authority has the power to provide immediate safety and protection for the child, authorised by a magistrate
- s. 46: police protection, i.e. police have the power to place a child in police protection for 72 hours

Courts are bound by the following key principles in making decisions regarding children:

- The child's welfare is paramount
- No order is to be made unless doing so will be in the child's interests
- Delays in legal proceedings are to be avoided
- The child's interests are protected by a duty on the court to complete a 'welfare checklist'

Orders available to the courts under the Children Act 1989 include the following:

- s. 16: Family Assistance Order – voluntary support to family
- s. 43: Child Assessment Order – court-authorised assessment of child's needs
- s. 31: Supervision Order – support to child at home
- s. 36: Education Supervision Order – support at home to ensure school attendance
- s. 38: Interim Care Order – provisional decision on child's future, placing child in care
- s. 31: Care Order – parental responsibility held by local authority, together with parents

In addition, in private law proceedings the court may make 's. 8 Orders', relating to:

- residence – replaces what was formerly custody order, confers parental responsibility on applicant

- prohibited steps – prevents person from taking child abroad; raising child in specified religion; or undertaking specific medical treatment

- contact – replaces 'access' in family proceedings

- specific issue – resolves dispute concerning child's medical treatment, education, religion or other contested issue

The issue of possible criminal prosecution is relevant here, although there is no specific law as such which sets out the crime of 'sexual abuse'. However, depending on the nature of the sexual molestation alleged, Maria's brother-in-law may have been liable to prosecution under the Sexual Offences Act 1956. This prohibits sexual intercourse between a man and a girl under the age of 16 years. If the girl is aged under the age of 13, the adult may be charged with an absolute offence, for which no defence is possible. If the girl is aged under 16 years, then certain defences are possible in law, such as believing that a marriage had taken place – perhaps under the legal system of another country – or the man is under 24 and genuinely believed the girl to be aged 16 (Gunn, 1996: 25). Alternatively, a criminal prosecution may be based on a charge of indecent assault or gross indecency.

The child has a role to play as a potential witness, in criminal proceedings, should they take place. Under s. 53 of the Criminal Justice Act 1991, children can be assumed to be competent witnesses, for example in cases involving sexual abuse or violence. Unless the court determines the child to be unreliable, based on the same criteria as would apply to an adult witness, then their evidence is treated with all seriousness by the court.

Following the recommendations of the Pigot Committee, which reported in 1989, children in abuse cases are now protected to some extent from the worst rigours of giving evidence in a court of law. The Pigot Committee recommended the preparation of children's evidence on video, and the use of 'live' video links in court, in order to spare the child witness the shock of coming face-to-face with the adult defendant in the courtroom. Many of these recommendations were put into practice with the Criminal Justice Act 1991. In some areas, there are witness support services for children giving evidence (Plotnikoff and Woolfson, 1996). *The Child Witness Pack* has also been developed by the NSPCC to prepare children for the process of giving evidence in court (NSPCC, 1993). The actual preparation of videos as evidence in court is governed by strict guidelines covering what is termed 'memorandum' interviewing, to avoid the use of leading questions, or undermining the value of the evidence in court (Home Office/Department of Health, 1992). Maria could, therefore, have been drawn into this process, having alleged abuse by her brother-in-law.

A major criticism of the process has been that, although the interviewing is a skilled and time-consuming task for social workers and police officers, the effort put into making the videos does not result in them being used widely or effectively in court. Even if the videos are used, few successful convictions of the alleged abusers are achieved as a result. The emotional stress on child victims of abuse, and on their parents, in making the videos is enormous. Appearing in court can also itself be an arduous experience for children, almost amounting to a reliving of the original abuse.

In addition, the legal processes involved in taking out a prosecution against the alleged abuser can lead to delays in the child receiving much needed therapeutic help. There is a strongly-held but mistaken view among professionals that the child must not receive therapy until *after* they have completed giving evidence in court; to do so would, it is argued, lead to the undermining of the child's evidence, on the basis that defending solicitors would then be able to claim that the child had been 'coached' in their replies by the interviewing social worker. Even where the social services are fully convinced of the urgent need for therapy for the child, it is claimed in some cases that such therapy requires prior authorisation by a reluctant Crown Prosecution Service.

This supposed ban on 'pre-trial therapy' is, in fact, a myth. The Home Office guidelines make this clear:

> Once the video recorded interview is complete, it should be possible for appropriate counselling and therapy to take place. It should become standard practice to inform the police and Crown Prosecution Service about the nature of any such therapy in each case. The defence may justifiably wish to know about both the nature and content of the therapy that has taken place before the child gives evidence in cross-examination. (Home Office/Department of Health, 1992: para. 3.44)

The Crown Prosecution Service (CPS) have made it clear that the CPS does not seek to operate such a ban, but simply advises caution about the possibly damaging effects of therapy on the prosecution case (Crown Prosecution Service, 1999). Policy varies from one area to another, depending on the attitude taken by the local CPS (SSI, 1994: 45–52). According to one experienced Crown Prosecutor, therapy is rarely advised against in their area. The advice is: 'if there is a requirement for therapy, don't ignore it, but always consult with us first . . . some forms of therapy don't affect the quality of the evidence and don't contaminate the evidence' (Jenkins, 1997b: 17). Play therapy, for example, may be seen to be helpful to the child in therapeutic terms, and yet not undermine the value of the child's evidence in court. However, group therapy – actually the type of therapy often preferred by children in this situation – may be much more problematic. Defending solicitors could claim that, after having taken part in group therapy, the child was confusing their own individual experiences with that of other victims, or was 'embroidering' their account in some other way as a result of this sharing of experiences (National Children's Home: Action for Children, 1994).

The implications for confidentiality with children need to be carefully thought through by the therapist in this situation. Provisional confidentiality may have resulted in the original suspected abuse being reported to the social services, under the relevant child protection guidelines. A case can be brought through the courts against the alleged abuser, either in the form of a criminal prosecution or via a civil case for damages, perhaps at a later stage. If this occurs, then the therapy given to the child can become part of the material considered by the court. Records of confidentiality and the therapist's recollections of the therapy can be called upon by the court to help decide the issues of guilt or liability involved. Therapists do not possess legal 'privilege' in these situations, although social work files may be protected by public interest immunity (Plotnikoff and Woolfson, 1995: 63). Under a court order or witness summons, highly sensitive personal information about the child's experiences can be exposed in court. The therapist should seek expert legal advice in this situation. One option is to approach the judge via a barrister to restrict access to therapeutic records to the absolute minimum necessary for deciding the case in hand (Jenkins, 1997a).

The development of the relationship between Maria and her male teacher, with its possibly predatory overtones, also raises legal issues concerning the protection of children. Although Maria did not necessarily perceive the relationship with him to be abusive, he was clearly in breach of his duty of trust to her as a pupil, in what must necessarily be an unequal relationship given the marked disparity in their ages. Following the proposed reduction in the age of consent for homosexual relationships to 16, Home Secretary Jack Straw has indicated the likelihood of legislation criminalising sexual relationships between teachers or others in a similar position of authority and young people under the age of 18 (*Guardian*, 22 June 1998). This is designed to protect vulnerable young people from abuse by persons in positions of trust. (Procedures for investigating allegations of abuse of children made against teachers are set out in Department for Education and Employment, 1995, Circular 10/95.) In this specific situation, it seems that little was done to protect Maria from this particular teacher, who was later promoted to take charge of pastoral care for the school as a whole.

THE RIGHTS OF CHILDREN AND OF PARENTS WITHIN THE CHILD PROTECTION PROCESS

The rights of these central groups once the process is begun are summarised below. Children have rights within the child protection process to:

- have their wishes and feelings considered, under the 'welfare principle';
- be party to legal proceedings, including the right to independent legal representation;
- act as a witness in legal proceedings, if judged to be competent by the court;
- give or refuse informed consent to medical examination (although this can be overridden by a court);
- make a complaint under s. 26 of the Children Act 1989;
- apply for Criminal Injuries Compensation;
- have qualified access to their own social work file.

Similarly, parental rights within the child protection process may be summarised as the right to:

- be involved in at least part of the case conference;
- know the name of the social worker responsible for the case, and how to contact them;
- know what the social workers will do, and what legal powers they hold;
- give or refuse explicit informed consent to a medical examination or interview (except where this conflicts with the rights of the child or with a prior court order);
- have qualified access to social work records;
- make a complaint under s. 26 of the Children Act 1989.

Sources: Lewis, 1992: 1–5; Smith, 1995: 125–6.

If working within a model of provisional confidentiality, the therapist may set in train the process of investigation and court action described earlier in the chapter. The child's rights within these processes are largely framed within the Children Act 1989 as being partly about welfare and protection from harm and partly about a right to participate to some degree in adult deliberations about their future. The therapist may, unwittingly, lose contact with the child at the point of reporting the abuse, as other professionals become more directly involved. Where the abuse is reported against the child's wishes, then, according to research findings from the

USA, it is the strength of the therapeutic relationship which determines whether the child will return to carry on working with the therapist (Levine et al., 1995: 117). The US experience also suggests that reporting can be useful in the short term, to the extent that it contributed to the reduction or prevention of further abuse in 80 per cent of cases studied (125). The longer-term effects on the child's sense of trust with adults may, however, be another matter. In Maria's case, reporting the abuse did not appear to protect her in the longer term from other potentially abusive relationships.

The implications for developing a child-centred form of therapy where the model is one of provisional confidentiality need to be carefully considered. Elements of good professional practice would include:

- discussing the proposed limits to confidentiality with the child at the earliest possible stage;
- sharing the need to report a specific incident or allegation with the child;
- working through the child's possible anger or resentment after making the report;
- providing follow-up where possible to renew contact with the child if this has been broken off.

(Adapted from Levine et al., 1995: 115–37.)

Following the report, the therapist may be drawn into a wider child protection arena, or even into acting as a witness in legal proceedings. The child clearly has a need for close support through the often traumatic processes of investigation and possible court action. Where this role is not taken on by social services or by another agency, then the possibility is that the therapist may begin to take on some of these activities – for example, by supporting the child in claiming Criminal Injuries Compensation for the abuse (Cobley, 1998; Plotnikoff, 1990). Where the practitioner begins to move out of their primary role as the child's therapist to that of *advocate*, there can be damaging effects on the actual therapeutic alliance, as described in the following text.

Therapeutic perspectives

The professionals who became involved in this case following disclosure were all sympathetic to Maria's situation and did as much as they felt possible in the particular circumstances to assist her. A mature male Greek Cypriot social worker was carefully selected to work with the family. Yet this was counter-productive in the event, as it seemed only to increase the family's sense of shame. The brother-in-law's flagrant ignoring of the police caution, whereby he continued to visit Maria's home, did not bring about any further responses by the police or social services. In addition, a report made to the education authority that Maria's teacher had been involved with a 14-year-old student produced nothing more than a warning for him, with a record of his behaviour being placed on the authority's files. Shortly afterwards he was promoted to a more senior position, which also gave him pastoral responsibility for the female students in the same school.

It would seem that an important motivating factor which often leads practitioners to disclose confidential information is the belief that, once action is taken, the child will be protected by agencies such as the social services, police child protection teams, and by members of the child's family. In more serious cases, the hope is that the alleged perpetrator will be removed from the family, allowing the child and remaining family members to live together in harmony. Certainly, in the case studies outlined, such events did not have this result. Instead, difficulties arose when the social services made an attempt to engage with the families, or when the police tried to carry out a prosecution. Indeed, there are well-known difficulties concerning prosecution, even in cases of sexual abuse, and successful convictions are rare. There are often valid and complex reasons for the lack of success in these interventions. Too few experienced professionals, decreasing financial resources and a lack of hard evidence are often cited as major factors. Yet it is beyond the scope of this work to evaluate in detail the role of the social services or police force, other than to state that the therapist who intervenes in the hope of satisfactory intervention by such agencies may be acutely disappointed in some situations.

There is often the hope that through intervention, the parents will support the child, causing family interactions to alter dramatically. But in the cases cited, it is clear that this is not always the outcome. The families in each situation strongly resisted all attempts to make use of the services which could have helped in facilitating such change and, it seemed, they could not be compelled to do so. It is perhaps unrealistic to hope that interventions through outside agencies – in the form of network meetings, placing the child's name on the child protection registers, prosecution and even conviction – can be successful in changing abusive patterns of behaviour within the family. Given the difficulties encountered by the professional agencies best equipped to deal with such interventions, it is clear that the therapist's own ability to change the child's external world is actually very limited indeed.

The therapist who seeks to change the child's external environment perhaps does so because, on the surface, this appears to be the simplest solution. The child who chose to have confidential treatment, however, was seeking an alternative solution. This is a form of change which only a competent therapist could provide: that of bringing about change in the child's internal world. For even supposing that interventions are successful on some occasions, and the perpetrator convicted of abuse is perhaps removed from the family, the question still remains: Who is going to work with the child's *internal* world? The difficulties for children in cases of abuse and neglect do not end either with failed interventions or with successful prosecutions, as neither can produce cures. To claim otherwise would suggest that only external situations influence the individual, and, as Anna Freud points out:

> In spite of accumulated evidence that adverse environmental circumstances have pathological results, nothing should convince the child analyst that alterations in external reality can work cures, except perhaps in earliest infancy. Such a belief would imply that external factors alone can be pathogenic agents and that their interaction with internal ones can be taken lightly. Such an assumption runs counter to the experience of the analyst. Every psychoanalytic investigation shows that pathogenic factors are operative on both sides, and once they are intertwined, pathology becomes ingrained in the structure of the personality and is removed only by therapeutic measures which effect the structure. (1966: 51)

Practitioners who intervene in the child's external world, entailing a loss of their role as therapist, may find it very difficult to later resume that role for the child concerned. When the external interventions have taken place, whether successful or not, it must be asked who will then be available to work exclusively with the child's internal world if the therapist has proved unable to do so?

Provisional confidentiality in therapy

In the case cited, it is clear that Maria found the rule of provisional confidentiality to be utterly confusing. Maria was informed at the outset that anything she said would be confidential, unless the therapist felt at any point that she might be in danger of some kind. As stated in Chapter 6, this type of contract not only inhibits what the client can discuss, it can also lead to a lasting and damaging degree of confusion. The client may not have a clear understanding of what material might be reported and what will remain confidential. Indeed, many therapists who are prepared to disclose client material in instances which indicate risk, often cannot agree among themselves which particular instances would lead them to do so. It seemed that Maria might have held the perception, when she disclosed the abuse by her brother-in-law, that the promise of confidentiality would remain intact; perhaps she may have thought the type of abuse might not be one of the 'dangerous' issues referred to by the therapist. Certainly it caused her a great deal of alarm when she found that this was to be reported, although this reporting was actually undertaken ultimately with Maria's express consent.

No doubt, therapists will often feel relieved of their own anxiety in this situation, yet there are two reasons why consent under such circumstances could be considered invalid. The first is that many clients, both adults and children, are readily prepared to please their therapists. Quite often the role of pleasing others has become customary in their lives; but it is the accepted duty of the therapist to assist in strengthening the client's ego to resist this role, rather than seeking to manipulate the client further. The client may also seek to please the therapist out of a fear of abandonment. Maria's need to please the therapist for these reasons may well have contributed to her eventually giving her consent, although with great reluctance. An additional factor which invalidates this consent is that the child concerned may not really understand what it is they are consenting to. This might be because the child cannot fully appreciate the real impact of having outside agencies involved in the family, of the possible arrest of the perpetrator, and/or of having to stand as a witness in court. Alternatively, the therapist cannot realistically inform the client of the outcome of disclosure in full detail, as this is not always, if ever, easily predicted.

In Maria's case, what she thought she was consenting to – as outlined by the therapist – was protection from abuse by her brother-in-law, the protection coming from outside agencies and from her family. This was only partially correct in that while the actual abuse stopped, Maria was not further protected from the perpetrator's psychological interference. Indeed, the outcome was far better predicted by the client than by the therapist, in that Maria's fears came to fruition as the family opposed her – with all the disharmony and upset that this entailed. Having lived through this experience, Maria was then able to gain a very clear understanding of the rules of provisional confidentiality. Maria's perception was that she could not fully discuss the relationship with her teacher, although this was clearly troubling her. To disclose such details would not result in therapeutic work designed to empower her, but would instead result in automatic reporting of child abuse. This in turn could lead to a court case and, this time, to possible total abandonment by her family.

It can only be assumed that child clients who are offered similar contracts of provisional confidentiality may have similar perceptions to those of Maria. In such situations, some children make an immediate decision to leave the therapeutic process, realising that they will be unable to discuss what is troubling them. Others will have a confused perception of what they are able safely to discuss, and may feel both bewildered and betrayed. For those children like Maria, who desperately want to be involved in a counselling process, a contract of provisional confidentiality may keep them in a constant state of internal conflict concerning who they want to talk to, what they want to talk about and what they feel safe to talk about.

The therapist as protector

The desire on the part of therapists to protect their clients is a powerful one, whatever the age of the clients. However, the compulsion to intervene in the external life of the client should be superseded by adherence to the therapeutic principle of empowering the client. Assuming even the best scenario from the child protection agencies in Maria's case, it might be hoped that the brother-in-law would never visit Maria's home or trouble her again. In addition, the education authority might have viewed the teacher's behaviour more seriously and disbarred him from the profession. While these protective measures would be highly commendable (and such protection would be supported by the therapist concerned), they would not leave Maria any better equipped to protect herself in similar situations which might arise. Child psychotherapist, Anne Alvarez, states that:

> Society's feeling that something is changed and resolved by the disclosure may not be shared by the child. What abuse has meant for him and meant to him may be very different from its meaning for us . . . our notions of protection, of justice, of care, may be quite unreal to him. (1992: 151–2)

Society's promised protection was somewhat unreal for Maria, who was far more consumed by her internal world. There seemed to be an unconscious motivating force, which made her vulnerable to a sexualised, abusive father figure. There was every possibility that she would embark upon relationships of the kind she had experienced with the teacher, whenever a similar figure emerged in the future.

The protection that therapists can offer comes from enabling clients to empower themselves through therapeutic treatment. In this case, the therapy would have allowed Maria to explore her internal world, with a strengthening of her ego, which might have resulted in her being able to protect herself in similar circumstances. It might be that in doing this Maria would have sought help from the police. However, that would have been her decision, and she would hopefully gain further strength from having carried through her decision. In this case, however, none of this was possible because the therapeutic alliance had broken down to the extent that Maria was unable to discuss anything of importance, either in her internal or external world.

If therapists are to preserve the therapeutic alliance and their own role as therapist, then the role of child protector as an external influence must be carefully thought through. This is not to suggest that children should not have the right to protection, if that is what they are asking for. However, it is important to listen carefully to children, particularly older children, in assessing whether it is protection they are asking for or a therapeutic service. In cases where the children are younger, and it might be reasonably assessed that the child is in need of protection, it is for therapists to ask themselves whether they are the only persons available in the child's life who can possibly initiate such protection. The role of child protection agent and therapeutic practitioner do not sit easily with each other. It is quite possible that the client will think of the therapist in the terms outlined by Langs in Chapter 2, as suffering from identity confusion. It is also possible that this perception will contain a deeper truth: that the therapist has not fully worked through his or her own ethical and professional stance on child protection – or on the question of the child's potential for autonomy.

8

Working with risk: the therapist as enabler

Case study: Harry

Harry, a highly intelligent white English boy, aged 12, was referred for therapy by his year tutor, for what was simply described as 'odd behaviour' (*sic*). It soon became apparent that Harry's symptoms were consistent with those of borderline psychosis, as classified in the Diagnostic and Statistical Manual, DSM-IV, under the subsection personality disorder. Having worked with many children in school settings over a number of years, this was the first time the therapist had encountered a child with possible borderline psychosis; as a result, supervision was sought with a highly experienced child psychotherapist who worked at a child guidance centre. It was the supervisor's usual practice to work with children and their families together. She indicated that Harry might experience a psychotic breakdown, and that the parents should be made aware of this possibility. The supervisor was concerned, and even somewhat alarmed initially, to learn that the parents were not actually aware that Harry was in therapy. The therapist had previously lost many clients, such as those discussed in the earlier case studies, through breaches in confidentiality, which had often led to negative interventions by parents. Harry had insisted from the outset of his therapy that he did not want his parents to know about his involvement in the process. At the time of working with Harry, the therapist had moved towards an approach which respected and upheld the child's wish for confidentiality in all cases. Yet, it was recognised that in some ways this was a case of a different nature. The ethical question of whether or not to inform Harry's parents about the extent of his disturbance, and that he would be in long-term treatment, became an issue of considerable importance.

During the following therapy session, it was suggested to Harry that perhaps his parents should be informed that he was engaged in therapy. Harry became visibly anxious. He began to tremble, saying he felt sure that his parents, in particular his father, would try to prevent him attending any further sessions. In Harry's own words, he felt his father 'would go ballistic'. Further insight was sought from the year tutor, who had referred Harry, about this issue. The tutor suggested that having met Harry's father, who she described as severely disturbed, she could fully understand Harry's anxieties. When it was suggested that the family could be referred together to attend child guidance, the year tutor felt that they would most likely refuse. She also shared Harry's belief that his father would try to stop the treatment altogether. In addition to being described as severely disturbed, it seemed that Harry's father was also a religious zealot who believed that all difficulties should be resolved only through the church. The opinion of another senior psychotherapist colleague was also sought. The colleague agreed that there was a possibility of breakdown, but there was also a possibility that, through therapy, Harry might simply get better.

Suggesting that his parents should be informed had caused Harry considerable distress, which he displayed throughout several sessions to follow. It was not until a clear assurance to Harry was offered, that no intervention would be made against his wishes, that he began to regain the trust that had previously been established in the therapeutic alliance. Harry remained in long-term therapy, never missing an appointment and he did, indeed, simply get better. Members of the teaching staff frequently commented on his much changed behaviour, and on his new-found ability to become increasingly in touch with reality.

Legal and practice perspectives

One possible outcome in this situation might have been for Harry to have received some form of psychiatric care. In most cases, this happens on what is called admission on a 'voluntary' or informal basis; of 7000 young people admitted for mental health treatment, 90 per cent were on such a voluntary basis (Alderson, 1994: i). Almost a fifth of psychiatric admissions of children are for those under the age of 10 (Department of Health, 1994: 50).

Provision for psychiatric treatment of young people under the age of 18 is set out in the *Code of Practice* for the Mental Health Act 1983. (The Act does not impose a legal duty to follow the Code, but it is noted that failure to do so 'could be referred to in evidence in legal proceedings' (Department of Health/Welsh Office, 1999: para. 1.1).) There is no minimum age set for admission to hospital under the Act. Fennell (1992, 1996) identifies three principles for the operation of the Act in relation to young people:

- they should be kept fully informed about their care and treatment;
- they should generally be regarded as being able to make their own decisions, with certain provisos;
- any intervention in the life of a young person should be 'the least restrictive possible'.

The legal situation regarding the treatment of young people under the age of 18, and under 16 in particular, is complex; it has also been affected by recent case law decisions and by the principles of the Children Act 1989. Parents or guardians of young people may agree to the admission of a young person under the age of 16 as an informal patient (see Table 8.1). Following

Gillick and later case law, 'where a "Gillick-competent" child wishes to discharge him or herself as an informal patient from hospital, the contrary wishes of any person who has parental responsibility will ordinarily prevail' (Department of Health/Welsh Office, 1999: para. 31.6). With young people aged 16–17, the young person may consent to treatment, but the refusal of a competent 16 or 17 year old to treatment may be overridden by a person with parental responsibility, or the courts.

It follows that Harry's parents could have agreed to his being admitted for psychiatric treatment as an informal patient, overriding his wishes, if thought necessary. In fact, although a matter of concern, Harry's behaviour never reached the stage of requiring psychiatric care. The therapist continued working with him in a confidential therapeutic relationship, the legal basis for which has been set out in Chapters 5 and 6.

In terms of children's rights, young people admitted on an informal basis do not have access to the formal protection available for those committed under a section of the Act. They do not qualify for automatic referral to a Mental Health Review Tribunal, nor do they come within the reporting scope of the Mental Health Act Commission (Children's Legal Centre, 1994b: 34). This represents a significant gap in the provision of rights and protection for children admitted as voluntary patients.

Psychiatric assessment for a child may be ordered by the courts, under s. 38 of the Children Act 1989, as part of an Interim Care Order. These

Table 8.1 *Summary of children's rights and parental responsibility for consent to informal admission, psychiatric treatment and discharge under the Mental Health Act 1983*

	Status of consent or refusal of consent for voluntary psychiatric treatment of children by persons with parental responsibility		
	Informal admission	Treatment	Discharge
'Gillick-competent' children under 16*	Parent may arrange child's admission. Parent cannot override child's wishes for admission.	Child may consent to treatment, but child's refusal of consent may be overridden by parent.	Child's wishes for discharge will be 'ordinarily' overridden by parent.
Children aged 16–17*	Child may arrange own admission, irrespective of parent's wishes.	Child may consent to treatment, but child's refusal of consent may be overridden by parent.	Child may discharge self, but use of compulsory treatment is a possible option.

*i.e. those deemed capable of expressing their own wishes

Source: Department of Health/Welsh Office (1999): 138–48

Orders normally last 8 weeks, but can be extended by the court. The assessment is subject to the agreement of the child, assuming that they are deemed to be 'Gillick-competent'. However, the child's refusal to consent can be overridden by the courts (South Glamorgan CC v. B and W [1993]).

A range of powers exist for authorising compulsory psychiatric assessment or treatment of children where these measures are thought to be needed. Children may receive compulsory psychiatric treatment under ss. 2, 3 and 4 of the Mental Health Act 1983 (see below for details of this Act). These sections are the main emergency provisions of the Mental Health Act 1983 and can be summarised as follows:

> s. 2: admission for assessment for a period of 28 days, authorised by two doctors, such as consultant psychiatrist and the patient's GP
>
> s. 3: admission for treatment, lasting 6 months, and extendable for a further 6 months, then reviewable on an annual basis by Mental Health Review Tribunal
>
> s. 4: emergency admission for 72 hours for assessment, usually authorised by the patient's GP and applied for by the patient's 'nearest relative' or an Approved Social Worker

Under the Mental Health Act 1983, medical treatment is taken to include physical treatment, such as the administration of drugs and Electro-Convulsive Therapy (ECT), and psychological treatment such as psychotherapy. The issues of professional competence and patient consent are emphasised in relation to the use of psychological treatment. (Department of Health/Welsh Office, 1999: para. 19.1).

The forms of psychiatric treatment available include:

> • medication
> • electro-convulsive therapy
> • group therapy
> • individual psychotherapy
> • behaviour modification

A crucial issue concerning medical and psychiatric treatment for children is that of consent. Children, as is the case with adults, need to give informed consent to treatment. Informed consent consists, first, of their capacity to understand the relevant issues and to make a free choice between alternative courses of action; and, second, the ability to give permission to a course of treatment. These features of informed consent may be summarised as follows:

> *Capacity*:
>
> - Understanding – client's understanding of costs, benefits and drawbacks of available alternatives
> - Choice – client's capacity to make a voluntary choice between alternatives
>
> *Consent*:
>
> - Permission – client's voluntary and continuing permission for their involvement based on their understanding (as outlined above)

Under s. 8 of the Family Law Reform Act 1969, children over 16 can give consent to medical treatment on the same basis as an adult. The *Gillick* decision extended this ability to give informed consent to those children under 16 who were seen to be of 'mature understanding'. *Gillick* was influential in the framing of procedures for the voluntary admission of children for psychiatric care, as set out in the first editions of the *Code of Practice*. However, recent dramatic case law has modified and weakened the impact of *Gillick* with regard to the provision of medical or psychiatric treatment for children, both for those under 16 and, in life-threatening situations, for children over 16 as well as seen in the 1999 edition of the *Code of Practice*.

There have been several key cases which have illustrated the limits of the child's right to give or to refuse consent for urgent medical treatment. In one case (*Re R* [1991]), a 15-year-old girl, with a history of severe behavioural problems, refused to take her anti-psychotic medication. The Court of Appeal decided that her refusal could be overridden, via alternative consent which was obtained either from her parents or authorised by the courts. Using the analogy of consent as a 'key' to unlock a door, Lord Donaldson argued that a competent minor could lock the door or refuse consent, but that other keyholders, such as parents or the courts, could unlock it and override the child's wishes (Urwin, 1992). Lord Donaldson later regretted the use of this analogy, as it still overstated the capacity of the young person to refuse treatment, for example by the use of the phrase 'locking the door' against medical help. He preferred instead the term 'flak jacket', by which he meant that the doctor or other person treating the young person only needed valid consent from one appropriate person, whether a '*Gillick*-competent' person under 16, a young person over 16, or a person with parental responsibility. The legal 'flak jacket' so obtained would then protect the doctor from any litigious claims at a later date (*Re W* [1992] at 767).

In a second case (*Re W* [1992]), a 16-year-old girl suffering from anorexia nervosa was moved, against her will, to a specialist treatment unit. The court decided that the *Gillick* decision did not mean that the rights of young people were absolute with regard to consent to treatment. In fact, W's views 'were of no weight' in the court's decision (Mulholland, 1993). In a third case (*Re C* (1997)), a 16-year-old girl suffering from a similar condition was also compelled to attend a specialist treatment clinic, under the powers of 'inherent jurisdiction' of the High Court (Frantz, 1997). However, once a child has reached the age of 18, they can then make drastic choices for themselves. In one situation, a boy aged 15, who was a Jehovah's Witness, refused to give consent for an urgent blood transfusion. This refusal to give consent was then overridden by the courts. Several years later, at the age of 18, he was able to then refuse a transfusion as an adult, despite the fatal consequences which ensued (*Re E* [1993]; *Re S* [1994]).

The law can, therefore, be used to override the child's wishes in critical situations, such as in the treatment of anorexia nervosa. The *Gillick* ruling has increased the child's right to make autonomous decisions, but it remains the case that this right can be overturned by the courts or person with parental responsibility in life-threatening situations. Thus, where a young person is refusing essential life-saving treatment, then their refusal to give consent can be overridden, if necessary, by obtaining the 'flak jacket' (referred to by Lord Donaldson) of valid consent given by someone with parental responsibility or by an order of the court. The effect of these judgements is reflected in the 1999 edition of the *Code of Practice* for the Mental Health Act 1983. The *Code* has been criticised by medical practitioners for restricting the rights of children formerly based on *Gillick* and limiting the professional discretion of doctors (Parkin, 1999).

The rights of children in psychiatric care can be summarised as the right:

- to give informed consent to treatment (subject to powers of the court, or those with parental responsibility);
- to decide on voluntary admission or discharge, if under 16, on the *Gillick* principle/Code of Practice (subject to powers of the court, or those with parental responsibility);
- to procedural protection as a patient, such as referral to a Mental Health Review Tribunal, if admitted on a 'section'.

The law regarding psychiatric care therefore provides an uneasy mix of respecting children's autonomy, via the *Gillick* principle affecting voluntary admissions, and more coercive elements, where parental consent or a court order can override the child's refusal of necessary treatment. The relevance to therapists of these rather complex and confusing cases is that they appear to limit the impact of the *Gillick* decision, and thus create an air of uncertainty for therapists working with children. Yet it needs to be borne in mind that these situations involved essential psychiatric treatment or life-threatening medical conditions. Here the courts have shown that they will not hesitate to intervene if necessary, to override the apparently self-destructive wishes of the child. The *Gillick* principle of children under 16 being capable of giving their informed consent remains true for the vast majority of such children who possess the ability to make a reasoned and informed choice about treatment, including therapy.

It may be useful to bear in mind some key reference points for medical and psychiatric treatment of children:

- s. 8, Family Law Reform Act 1969
- ss. 2, 3, 4, Mental Health Act 1983
- *Gillick* decision by House of Lords [1986]
- ss. 8, 38, 100, Children Act 1989
- case law – *Re R* [1991]; *Re W* [1992]; *Re C* (1997)
- Mental Health Act 1983: Code of Practice (1999)

Risk of self-harm

One possibility might have been for Harry to receive either voluntary or compulsory psychiatric treatment under the Mental Health Act 1983. This did not come about because the therapist chose to work with him individually, deciding that he possessed capacity and was able to consent to continuing work. The school's policy of protecting therapeutic confidentiality with pupils did not require prior parental permission (see Chapter 5). However, working with children with a possible psychotic illness presents a great deal of risk for all parties, including the child, their parents, the rest of the family, the therapist and the agencies directly involved.

One set of risks relates to the possibility of 'deliberate self-harm' or of suicide. Deliberate self-harm includes para-suicide, deliberate self-poisoning and attempted suicide, and is predominantly undertaken by girls and women, with an increasing rate evident among older adolescent girls. Suicide rates, in contrast, show a continuing increase among young males, with young men being three times more likely than young women to commit suicide (Williams and Morgan, 1994: 49). For young men in the 15 to 24 age group, there was a 60 per cent increase in suicide in the period

1986 to 1991. The risk figures take on additional significance when supported by other data which illustrate the isolation from possible sources of support which is experienced by many young people. A survey carried out by the Samaritans of more than 8000 14–17-year-olds in North London found that:

- 18 per cent felt they had no one to talk to in a crisis;
- 43 per cent had felt, at times, that there was no point in living;
- 11 per cent had attempted suicide;

as reported in an issue of *Childright* (Children's Legal Centre, 1994a: 15).

Therapists need to assess a client's risk of committing deliberate self-harm or suicide, in many therapeutic situations. Assessment of suicide risk may be based on consideration of the following (adapted from Williams and Morgan, 1994: 57):

- *Risk factors* – alcohol or substance abuse, bullying, being in custody, experience of physical or sexual abuse;
- *Preoccupation* – evidence that the person is currently thinking about death or suicide;
- *Trigger* and *means for suicide* – current stressful events, availability of means for suicide;
- *Support* – family and other key relationships, and whether they are capable of providing emotional support.

In the event, Harry did not appear to be a high risk either for deliberate self-harm or for a suicide attempt. The perceived risk was perhaps more of him undergoing a psychotic episode if he was unable to cope with previously unconscious material becoming more accessible – but also less easily containable – via the therapeutic process. Despite his bizarre ideas, he remained highly committed to the therapeutic work, and gradually showed some improvement in terms of his ability to relate to others in his peer group and to the teaching staff at school. However, if he had experienced a psychotic breakdown or had engaged in behaviour putting himself or others at risk, the outcome for himself and for the therapist would have been very different. In a case of suicide, a therapist may be called to give evidence at the Coroner's Court, and to be cross-examined on their professional skills and qualifications to work with disturbed teenagers. Legal action in the form of the aggrieved parents suing the school or the therapist is perhaps less likely to happen. However, to minimise personal and professional risk, the therapist in this situation needs carefully to consider:

- their own level of expertise and training;
- their level of confidence and competence in working with clients at higher risk of deliberate self-harm or suicide;
- the level, frequency and adequacy of professional supervision and consultation;
- professional indemnity insurance cover;
- access to accurate legal advice;
- familiarity with and commitment to relevant professional codes of practice;
- clear agency policy and guidelines on confidentiality, and on working with risk to self or to a third party;
- clear contracting with the client about confidentiality and any limits that apply.

In working with Harry, the therapist was able to consider and work with these factors, contributing towards a positive outcome for the client.

Therapeutic perspectives

The term 'borderline psychosis' was adopted by the therapist here as a useful working concept in Harry's therapy, in that it accurately captured some of the key aspects of his experience, behaviour and overall level of personal distress. However, as a term it is somewhat problematic, given the immediate objection that such a diagnosis is only for a properly qualified psychiatrist to make in the first instance. There is, to start with, variation between psychiatrists in their own understanding and use of the term (Freeman, 1993: 605). In addition, the concept is often used in a rather different sense by psychoanalysts, where an individual may be seen as operating along a shifting continuum between neurosis and psychosis (Alvarez, 1992: 108). Also, the classifications used in the UK diagnostic manual ICD-10 (World Health Organisation, 1992) and its US equivalent, DSM-IV (American Psychiatric Association, 1994), are not always easily comparable and, crucially, refer to <u>adults</u> rather than to children (Wolff, 1993: 84). The concept, despite these qualifications, proved to be useful to the therapist in gaining an understanding of the nature of Harry's experience.

The main features of borderline personality disorder (as defined in DSM-IV) are:

- impulsivity
- ·unpredictability, with unstable but intense interpersonal relationships
- uncertain identity

- unstable mood
- fear of being alone
- self-damaging behaviour

Source: American Psychiatric Assocation, 1994: 280–1

All of these features, with the exception of self-damaging behaviour, were evident in this situation. Harry frequently exhibited unpredictable behaviour, with frequent rapid changes from a quiet and passive mood to fits of rage. Such outbursts would often take place in the classroom, where he would tip over desks and chairs. At home he would, as he put it, 'smash up his room'. Of this he would say, 'afterwards it looks like a poltergeist has been in there'. Harry also experienced unstable but intense interpersonal relationships, most particularly with his father. He would often express hatred of his father, yet the intensity of this key attachment relationship was also clear. Harry felt that somehow he and his father were, as he put it, 'inside each other' and that he would inevitably inherit his father's worst characteristics. He also demonstrated the feature prominent in borderline psychosis of having an uncertain identity. In this, he presented himself as feeling half-alive, half-dead. His mind wandered up in space, with endless tales of astronauts, or back in history, with accounts of the lives of Garibaldi, Galileo, Einstein and Hitler. He had little identity as a 12-year-old boy, and shared no interests in the everyday activities of his peers. Harry also frequently expressed his fear of being alone, once saying that, throughout his life, it felt 'as though there was just him and four walls'.

During sessions, Harry's sentences were often incoherent, containing a series of loose associations. There was nothing that preceded or followed statements such as 'the grass is always greener in England' or 'if two people swapped over brains everyone would know inside ten minutes'. These statements made no sense, given their lack of context, yet Harry was by no means unintelligent. In the classroom, he alternated between the boy who kicked over furniture and frightened his peers and a quiet bespectacled, soberly dressed individual who achieved A grade passes in his exams. In the sessions, among the loose associations, there were also statements that were coherent, sometimes profoundly intelligent, and frequently moving. While his interest in space and history constantly took him away from reality, the historical details he was able to discuss were nevertheless considerable for a child of his age. He was also adept at describing his feelings of despair, making statements such as, 'I feel like I'm a piece of Swiss cheese, and every hole represents something bad someone has done to me'. It could not be overlooked that one of the statements which was made with extreme clarity was his belief that his father would 'go ballistic' if he was told about the therapy, and would stop Harry from attending.

In working with Harry the usual techniques of psychotherapy were not of primary importance. Any attempt to make transference interpretations only seemed to alarm Harry. Psychotherapists familiar in working with psychotic clients, such as Le Boit, advocate that emphasis should be on interventions rather than interpretations (1979). The usual language of psychotherapy had to be suspended when working with Harry. It was pointless to use such phrases as 'I wonder where your thoughts have gone to'; this would only evoke responses such as that given on one occasion: 'they've gone across time and space'. Karon says of his psychotic patients, 'They believe I talk funny, because I do talk funny. In fact, so do all therapists because of our technical vocabulary' (1987: xx).

What did become of major importance in this work was that the therapeutic structure and alliance was maintained, and that the client was really listened to. Harry announced during one session: 'I look at myself in the mirror and I think, I despise you, I'm a blank and no one takes me seriously or listens to me'. It seemed that if Harry was ever going to improve it was vital that someone should begin both to listen to him and to take him seriously. This also applied to his explicit wish for confidentiality.

Balancing risks and benefits in therapeutic work

In this case, the child client did get better, but at the beginning of therapy there was no certainty that this would happen. There was a considerable risk that Harry could have experienced a psychotic breakdown, perhaps requiring admission to a psychiatric unit. This potential scenario proved to be very anxiety-provoking for the therapist. This anxiety was heightened by the knowledge that the therapist's decision not to involve Harry's parents was, for a time, questioned by a far more experienced and senior supervisor. The supervisor subsequently gave some thought to the contrasting approach of working only with individual child clients in isolation, compared to the more common practice at the child guidance clinic of working with the whole family; the latter approach had not previously led to the question being raised of offering confidential treatment to the child without parental involvement. When the supervisor reflected on this issue, the case discussed here was followed with great interest – and with keen surprise and acknowledgement of the eventual positive outcome. The supervisor's colleague at the clinic, another experienced child psychotherapist, also began to question the automatic reporting back to parents of each session's content when working with individual children. A particular case, where a mother had been intrusive in this way, had caused concern. The psychotherapist had not given real thought to the application of the *Gillick* principle to therapeutic work with children. Both practitioners then began to question their way of working, which they had previously taken for granted.

Had the worst scenario come about, there is little doubt that Harry's parents would have shown their disapproval of the therapy being provided without first obtaining their consent. Yet the alternative action, that of breaching confidentiality and involving Harry's parents, also involved considerable risks. Harry gave a good indication, supported by the year tutor, that his parents would have tried to prevent him from attending further sessions. Had such a situation arisen, it is possible that this might have eventually resulted in an application for a 'specific issue order' under the Children Act 1989 (see Chapter 5). The court might have decided that it was in Harry's best interests to continue in therapy. However, alternatively the court may not have viewed a possibly borderline psychotic child such as Harry, as necessarily qualifying as '*Gillick*-competent'. Yet the definition of 'competence' is based on the child demonstrating a sufficient maturity and level of understanding to decide about their own need for confidential treatment. It would have been difficult to argue that Harry was not highly intelligent, as he had gained A grades in examinations. However, his incoherent language towards the beginning of his treatment could, nevertheless, have perhaps led the court to believe, wrongly, as it happened, that he was *not* capable of using this intelligence to make an appropriate decision about remaining in therapy.

Another major risk in breaking confidentiality in this case was the possible damage to the therapeutic process. Harry's level of anxiety was such that it was felt that he could not have endured opposition to the therapy coming from his parents. He would almost certainly not have coped well with any involvement by the courts or other agencies. In addition, the therapeutic alliance played an important role in Harry's treatment, as it was vital for him to trust fully the person to whom he had decided to disclose the more frightening aspects of his personality. Having witnessed less emotionally vulnerable clients leaving therapy as an indirect consequence of breaches in confidentiality, the therapist was all too aware that a similar breach of confidentiality could have a serious impact on the therapeutic alliance. In this case, the risks for both parties, therapist and client, were considerable. However, the anxiety was contained, affording Harry the opportunity for successful treatment.

The therapist as enabler

The role of therapy as a structure for containing the child's anxiety and phantasy is emphasised by Alvarez:

> The reliability and regularity provided by the psychoanalytic setting – the child
> in the same room at the same time – and the firm structure of psychoanalytic

technique provide an opportunity for structure and order to begin to develop in the child's mind. The results of this opportunity for 'containment' are particularly striking with very ill, borderline psychotic, sexually abused children or deprived children. (Alvarez, 1992: 4)

In the case of Harry, as previously outlined, it was not the more usual applications of psychoanalytic technique that were of primary importance. What was important was the provision of a firm structure, one in which Harry could feel safe and sufficiently contained to work through his internal difficulties within the therapy setting. As advocated by Alvarez, the sessions were held in the same room and at the same time, every week for over two years. Equally important to this structure was a firm contract of confidentiality, which was upheld throughout the treatment process. This not only provided Harry with a firm basis of security but also meant that, instead of adopting various roles, the therapist could strictly carry out the function of 'enabler'. Some order did begin to develop in the client's mind. Harry's fits of rage, both at home and in the classroom, diminished and his relationships with his peers greatly improved. They no longer feared the boy who used to wreck the classroom or would try to engage them in nonsensical conversations. Instead, they were able to see Harry as a thinking, sensitive and capable human being. Towards the end of his treatment, Harry was voted form captain by his peers – a position awarded to the most well liked and responsible student in the class. His teachers commented on his ever-increasing ability to remain in touch with reality, to engage in meaningful conversations, and on his new-found ability to maintain eye contact.

Ellen, Natalie, Maria and Harry were children who all fell within the categories outlined by Alvarez, namely children who were deprived, abused or borderline psychotic. They all sought help through a therapeutic process but, in the event, it was perhaps the most unlikely client of the four who was actually helped through this process. It could be argued that this was because Harry's difficulties were psychological, and therefore of an internal nature, whereas those of the other clients were mainly due to external causes. It would perhaps follow that it was therefore appropriate to address problems of an internal nature through therapy, while those caused externally could only be dealt with through more direct forms of intervention, such as the reporting of child abuse. Yet it would be an error to believe that all Harry's difficulties were internal and all those of the other clients were somehow external in origin. There may have been something in Harry's constitution which made him vulnerable to his particular disorder, although he was treated successfully without medication of any kind.

What did emerge throughout his therapy was that Harry had experienced a profoundly difficult relationship with his parents. In the case of Maria, the client's difficulties did not end when her brother-in-law stopped sexually abusing her. Something had become internalised, which contributed to her being vulnerable to involvement in a sexual relationship with a much older adult male. Harry was enabled through therapy to gain greater self-awareness, and thus to approach relationships from a different standpoint. There was nothing to prevent the other clients in these cases from reaching a similar level of self-awareness, had they been given the opportunity to do so. By maintaining the role of enabler, the therapist may have been able to help move these clients towards a position of empowerment, from which they could have brought about changes in their external environments. These may have ultimately come about either partly through interventions by the social services or the police or, more significantly, as a result of their own autonomous decision making if they had decided to contact the authorities on their own behalf. Such an approach would not have interfered with the therapeutic process, which could then have successfully focused on the client's internal world.

The opportunity for the therapeutic work to operate in this way did not arise in the earlier examples. It was difficult to establish order in the lives of these clients, given that the therapeutic process was not ordered in itself and did not offer a firm, containing structure for the clients. The practitioner moved from the role of therapist to those of mediator, law enforcer and child protector, and back again. More importantly, the therapeutic structure contained only an illusion of confidentiality and was based on real breaches of trust. The prognosis for a successful outcome in the case of Harry was no more likely than in these other cases. Given that it was the same therapist working with Harry as with the other clients, what was crucially different was the approach taken towards keeping confidentiality. The therapist had moved from offering a contract of provisional confidentiality, to that of maintaining complete confidentiality throughout treatment. In these case studies, it was this factor above all which contributed to a positive outcome, compared to the earlier responses, which failed to meet the needs of the children involved as clients.

Part 3 THERAPY WITH CHILDREN – SOME CONCLUSIONS

9

Empowering children

The previous chapters have attempted to explore professional dilemmas within therapy, and relate them directly to the law and to concepts of best practice. The theme of this book has been to endorse the child's rights as client in therapy, and to promote the rights of the child under the law to confidentiality within the therapeutic relationship. Both aspects interact and fuse together within the overall process of empowering children within therapy. The concept of empowerment within therapy has been heavily influenced by feminism, but extends to embrace a wide range of groups disadvantaged by society. McWhirter uses the term to include the following clients:

(a) the client has been identified as a member of a specific powerless group . . . ;
(b) the control gained in counseling has an impact on the client's life context at personal, interpersonal, and societal levels . . . and;
(c) the traditional power differential maintained in the therapy is altered in the direction of increased equality between counselor and client. (1991: 224)

In many ways it can be seen that children lack power, both within the wider society and within the therapeutic relationship itself. Therapists can counteract this imbalance of power within the working alliance by offering real choices to children and by maintaining confidentiality as a secure framework for the therapeutic work to be carried out. From an ethical point of view, empowerment is consistent with the principle of promoting the client's individual autonomy and, thus, their potential for self-determination. Empowerment needs to be addressed by therapists in their work with children for the following three main reasons.

First, children need to be treated as individuals. The child's capacity for mature reflection, understanding and decision making will depend upon their individual personality, life experience, degree of emotional stability and level of cognitive understanding. Their capacity for decision making needs to be explored and assessed in each individual situation. The therapist who works on the basis of assessment of the child's capacity for decision making being determined by chronological age is failing to acknowledge the real potential of the actual child facing them.

Second, each child needs to develop skills and experience in making decisions for themselves, in order to learn to cope with life's problems and to develop further as a person. The therapist can help in this process of development by enabling them to explore options and outcomes for the difficult decisions they encounter. The more practice that a child has gained in taking responsibility for making these choices, the better prepared they will be for adulthood. Therapists thus help the child to move towards self-actualisation, to realise their potential for choice and responsibility and assist in preparing them for adulthood.

Finally, despite significant changes in the law, most structures and processes in society continue to be more firmly based on principles of welfare and control than on those of promoting children's autonomy. The therapeutic space offered in a counselling context may be one of the few opportunities for the child to take stock of his or her life, to make connections and to move forward. The respect that is offered here can provide a crucial stimulus for the child to gain a stronger sense of self and to build their self-esteem in an otherwise unsupportive environment.

Children's rights

The longest and most established therapeutic model for work with children derives from psychoanalysis, although many of the core principles are applicable to other approaches, such as the person-centred and cognitive behavioural models. The psychoanalytic approach, with its requirement for a secure and consistent therapeutic frame, places particular emphasis on the need to work with the child as the client. Involving parents or other adult authority figures may mean that the child's freedom to reveal very sensitive or personal material is held in check because of the possible consequences of disclosure to others, as in the case of Maria described in Chapter 7. For the therapist to suddenly shift to take on the additional roles of mediator with other agencies, law enforcer or child protector may result in alienation of the child involved. Such moves undermine the therapy with external influences, and reveal a serious degree of confusion about the therapist's own professional role and purpose. This is not to say that a therapist would necessarily just sit back and do nothing in the case of immediate and unequivocal danger to a child. Nor is it intended to dismiss the difficult role of child protection workers in a casual or unsympathetic manner. However, the actual risk of continuing child abuse is often not clear-cut. The available alternative options for the child to obtain help, or for other interested parties to intervene, may be all too easily overlooked. The familiar argument that the child only reveals abuse to the therapist with the unconscious intention that the therapist should take action to prevent it may be true in some situations. However, it minimises the child's capacity for conscious choice. It also provides a convenient blanket rationalisation for the therapist's decision to break confidentiality with the child.

A second line of argument concerns the rights held by the child within society as a whole. Empowerment requires that the therapist is aware of the wide range of situations where children have rights, in the sense of a claim to treatment under law or policy. Children have rights under international law regarding the provision of services, protection from harm and exploitation, and participation in decision making. These rights are further strengthened by a raft of entitlements under statute, case law and codes of practice. Sadly, these rights are too often completely unknown to the child and/or imperfectly grasped by the professionals working with them. The therapist may be unaware of the child's rights or may opt, automatically, to include parents within the therapeutic framework as standard procedure. In doing so, they may be acting from the ethical standpoint of 'self-interest' and 'beneficence', rather than from the perspective of 'autonomy and self-determination'. The therapist may well be implicitly offering the child an adult-centred version of therapy, rather than the child-centred alternative which, arguably, would be better suited to the child's needs.

Ethical choices of therapists

The therapist needs to decide whether to work within a framework of parental oversight of therapy, provisional confidentiality or absolute confidentiality. Without a clear choice, the therapist may be acting without thinking through the implications, in terms of either the rights of the child concerned or the potential effects on the therapy itself. From a psychoanalytic perspective, the most robust defence of the case for absolute therapeutic confidentiality has been made by writers such as Christopher Bollas. He argues passionately that, within the analytic tradition, clients need the 'freedom to free associate', railing against the pervasive mandatory reporting laws and their damaging effects on therapeutic practice in the US and UK: 'proponents of the reporting laws place the legal system's hunger for information before the aims of psychotherapy and the confidentiality that makes it possible to achieve them' (Bollas and Sundelson, 1995: 55). This is a powerful case in the context of analytic work with adults. The emotional and physical vulnerability of children to abuse and harm will be an additional factor that therapists need to take into account in considering the application of Bollas's arguments to their work, whatever their theoretical orientation.

In order to empower their clients, therapists need to know and understand both their own rights and the rights of others. In the case of Ellen, described in Chapter 4, the Local Education Authority capitulated all too quickly to the parent's demands that counselling be ended forthwith. This appears to have been an example of a classic administrative response. The LEA perceived the situation purely in terms of their duties and liabilities as a local authority, combined with an outdated notion of parental rights. The voice of the child – as an independent party in this conflict – was entirely absent. This situation parallels that of social work before the Children Act 1975, where the child's right to participate in decision making was overlooked in law. It is revealing that the few children's rights officers in existence are appointed within social services departments. Arguably, they are equally needed in school settings, where the culture is much more resistant to the concept of children's participation and autonomy.

While this may still be a grey area of the law, with little to go by in terms of actual case law, it is arguable that a firmer knowledge of the legal principles involved and a consequently more robust response – by the therapist and by the authorities – might well have produced a different outcome. It seems apparent that a lack of knowledge of the legal context within which they operate is not uncommon among therapists in the UK. Yet it seems unlikely that therapists can best serve their clients without having at least a basic knowledge and working understanding of the law, in order to protect their work and to preserve the fragile therapeutic space within which they operate. Therapists increasingly need a basic grasp of the law as it applies to their practice, and an awareness of how to obtain speedy and accurate legal advice when required.

The power of the individual therapist may well be a significant but largely unacknowledged factor in their work with children. First there is inequality here in terms of age, experience and professional status; in addition the therapist has the capacity to shape and influence the work, its process and outcomes, in crucial ways. Therapists need to consciously address their own use or abuse of power in working with children. The ladder of participation, outlined in Chapter 1, points out some of the dangers in ascribing to the child in therapy a role which is purely token-istic, rather than one which can develop their potential for developing a degree of control and real participation in the therapeutic process. As anti-discriminatory practice takes a firmer hold of therapists' training and practice, it becomes increasingly important for therapists to examine their own use of power within their therapeutic work.

It has been a constant background factor in this discussion that the options available to therapist and client are heavily, indeed even over-whelmingly, influenced by the nature of the setting in which they practice. The rights of children vary significantly according to the context in which they are situated. Many of the rights of children to take part in decision making, without necessarily having a deciding say in the outcome, apply within a social work setting (as outlined in the Chapter 1). The child's rights to make autonomous decisions, subject to adult confirmation, often derive from a health care setting due to the *Gillick* decision. The sphere of education stands apart from this wider social influence as an enclave where the child's rights even to take part in decision making, let alone influence the outcome, are severely constrained. In each case, the context will have a major influence on what the therapist sees as realistic or possible in working independently with the child as client. The inconsistencies in law and entitlement between one setting and another may also undermine the therapist's confidence in upholding the rights of the child, and in challenging ways in which these rights are overlooked or infringed upon by other parties.

This brings the discussion onto the *Gillick* decision. More than a decade after this landmark legal decision and crucial piece of case law, it stands as a rather battered and chipped monument, where the inscriptions are weather beaten and somewhat hard to read. Arguably, the impact of the *Gillick* decision on society is still yet to be fully felt. It is debatable, for example with regard to children's autonomy, whether the Children Act 1989 was more strongly influenced by the *Cleveland Report's* recommendations for children's participation in decision making than by *Gillick*, which promoted the concept of the child's autonomous right to confidential medical advice and treatment. The earlier enthusiasm of groups such as the Children's Legal Centre for *Gillick* in endorsing the child's right to confidential counselling now seems somewhat more muted and hedged around with qualifications a decade later (Children's Legal Centre, 1989a: 12, 1997, 3–4).

Perhaps part of the problem with advancing children's rights under *Gillick* is that it is much more an issue of *values* and *attitudes* than it is simply of law or information about entitlement. As Alderson and Montgomery found in their research into non-urgent health care choices by children, adults' attitudes towards the participating children's capacity to make choices was much more determined by the adult's particular disposition to trust the child than by other more supposedly rational factors. In other words, crucially, 'each adult's view about competence seemed determined less by training or logic than by a disposition to trust or control children' (Alderson and Montgomery, 1996: 47). In a society which is seemingly reluctant to promote the wider participation and autonomy of children, it may be that the real work needs to be done with adults' gut-feelings and values, alongside the more cognitive processes of informing adults about children's rights to treatment under the law.

Part of the unclear legacy of *Gillick* lies in the attempts to limit its impact, through subsequent case law restricting the rights of children. These have been applied in cases of children under 18 years of age, as well as those under 16, who were refusing consent to urgent or life-saving medical treatment. The effect of these individual, and somewhat exceptional, cases may have been to blunt the overall impact of *Gillick*. They suggest that the principle of a child under the age of 16 being able to access confidential advice and treatment no longer applies quite so strongly. The adoption of the term 'Gillick-competent' can also be misleading in itself, through the subtly limiting effects of language. This term implicitly restricts the child's competence to a specific and narrowly defined medical sphere. In contrast, the law clearly acknowledges the child's legal 'competence' in a wide range of other significant areas such as instructing a solicitor in family cases, in acting as a witness in criminal or civil cases, or in initiating legal action under the Children Act 1989.

The difficulties in implementing Gillick are perhaps tied up with the internal inconsistencies of the decision itself. The two Law Lords, Fraser and Scarman, used different approaches in reaching their conclusion that a child of mature understanding was entitled to a confidential relationship with their doctor. These are described respectively as a 'welfare' versus a 'legal capacity' approach by de Cruz (1987). Lord Fraser's argument rested on the view that there were no grounds under statute for rejecting the capacity of a person aged under 16 to decide on their own medical treatment. In addition, there were established grounds in law for a doctor treating a child without first seeking parental consent. Finally, parental rights were increasingly seen in society as being relative, rather than absolute and fixed for all time: the law, therefore, needed to reflect these wider social changes. Lord Scarman's approach was more wide-ranging, in searching for the legal principle underlying previous case law, namely that parental rights were derived solely from duties towards the child. The most telling part of his case was the placing of the debate in a much wider social and historical context. In this he included the changing role of women, the moves towards greater access to and acceptance of the use of contraception, and the decreasing significance of fixed age limits for determining rights and entitlements for young people. Rather than seeing the case as being about an apparently technical problem which had arisen about medical confidentiality, Lord Scarman directly addressed the broader canvas of social change which provided the essential backdrop to the immediate issue: 'The law relating to parent and child is concerned with the problems of growth and maturity of the human personality . . . the law must be sensitive to human development and social change' (Gillick v. West Norfolk AHA [1985] at 421). Anticipating the charge that the new approach to the law would generate uncertainty regarding its application, he responded that 'uncertainty is the price which has to be paid to keep the law in line with social experience' (at 425).

Lord Scarman's arguments not only provide ringing judicial authority for confidential treatment for children under 16 who possess a sufficiently mature understanding to give informed consent; his reasoning also places this change in the law in the context of wider social change. This requires the law to keep pace and reflect these changes, or risk becoming seen as irrelevant and obsolete. The opportunities opened up by the Gillick decision have, in turn, been met by later case law endorsing the notion of parental 'veto' to childhood autonomy in extreme life-threatening situations. According to Lord Donaldson, 'good parenting involves giving minors as much rope as they can handle, without an unacceptable risk that they will hang themselves' (*Re W* [1992] at 638).

Buried somewhere in this stark metaphor concerning 'rope' is an association of harm arising from too much freedom for the young and of the burden of self-responsibility proving too heavy to bear. Pursuing the metaphor slightly further, however, rope has many other constructive uses – it can be used to link people together, to support others and to strengthen structures. The underlying message here seems to be that the developing autonomy of young people is to be perceived as a threat to the social order, rather than as an opportunity to harness. In contrast to the idea of rope as a brutal means of self-destruction, Winnicott provides some alternative ways of exploring this metaphor. From his own practice, he describes several situations where children used string in creative and therapeutic ways to convey complex notions of separation and connectedness (1974: 18–21, 50). Metaphor, as always, suggests the underlying values and attitudes, here concerning the child's real potential for growth and autonomy.

The conflicting messages about *Gillick* and following it were amplified by an outgoing Conservative government that had overseen a trebling of child poverty during its period in office. The previous government's reforms in education, as has been argued earlier, conflicted with the bi-partisan welfare orientation of the Children Act 1989. Parental consumer choice was to be the driving force of educational change, with no place for children's rights within the school gates. A token of the lukewarm official support for the UN Convention on the Rights of the Child was shown by the contrast between the 50,000 copies of the Convention that were distributed and the 20 million copies of the Parents Charter for Education – rather a poor comparison. On the issue of sex education, it almost seemed at one point that covert warfare raged between opposing government departments. In 1994 the Health Minister ordered the pulping of 15,000 copies of the *Pocket Guide to Sex* for children on the grounds of it being too 'smutty'. The differences between the Departments of Health and Education seemed to be sharply contrasted over the question of sex education; as described in Chapter 4, official Department for Education and Employment Circulars stressed the restrictions and potential legal dangers of teachers giving advice on sexual matters. On the other hand, the Department of Health was busy giving sympathetic acknowledgement of the particular needs of young gays and lesbians in local authority care (Bremner and Hillin, 1993: 58–65). One significant parting shot of the departing government, in its White Paper on the reform of social services, seemed to be reserved for the alleged excesses of *Gillick*. Accordingly, the government did not believe that emphasising the interests of the individual child should be allowed to become an excuse for distorting the proper relationship between children and adults . . . (it is) important not to ascribe to children the capacity to make the mature judgements about their interests which are the proper responsibility of adults. (Department of Health/Welsh Office, 1997, para. 3.3)

Referring here to the implicit concepts of 'proper relationships' and 'proper responsibilities', both left unclarified, suggests an inbuilt resistance to change on these matters.

It may be unfair to single out a former government for its dilatory attitude to children's rights, as it may be much more to do with society's overall ambivalence on the issue. After all, change on significant issues has often come about through the influence of external bodies on the UK. Corporal punishment in state schools was ended following a judgement in the European Court of Human Rights, and the principle of children's (and adults') more open access to files was established via the same route. The pending restrictions on a parent's common law right to use 'reasonable chastisement' in punishing their child has lately been challenged in a similar manner. Perhaps in some senses the *Gillick* decision – with its attendant rights for children and young people – was actually somewhat in advance of popular understanding or approval.

If this is the case, it may well fall to therapists working with children to pick up the challenge of these issues more strongly. Therapists occupy a particular position in society, working with those who are stigmatised and rejected by society, those who feel acute distress or those who have been devalued in devastating ways. In this sense, therapists perhaps operate at the very cutting edge of society's values, working both with vulnerable individuals and with often profoundly uncomfortable issues. In promoting the right of children to confidentiality within therapy, supported by a growing set of substantial rights within society, therapists may ultimately be doing no more than returning to their original roots.

Appendix: Relevant organisations

Association of Child Psychotherapists, 120 West Heath Road, London N3 7TU; 0208 458 1609; 0208 458 1482 (fax); acp@dial.pipex.com

Association of Lawyers for Children, PO Box 2029, Buckhurst Hill, Essex IG9 6EQ; 0208 505 3900 (tel/fax)

Childline, Royal Mail Building, Studd Street, London N1 0QN; 020 7239 1000; 020 7239 1001 (fax); 0800-1111 (Helpline) 0800-884444 (Children in care); www.Childline.org.uk

Children's Legal Centre, University of Essex, Wivenhoe Park, Colchester, Essex CO4 3SQ; 01206 873820; 01206 874046 (fax); www2.essex.ac.ux/clc

Children's Rights Alliance, 319 City Road, London EC1V 1LJ; 0207 278 8222; 0207 728 9552 (fax)

Council for Disabled Children, 8 Wakley Street, London EC1V 7QE; 0207 843 6000

Counselling in Education, c/o British Association for Counselling, 1 Regent Place, Rugby, Warwickshire CV21 2PJ; 01788 550899; 01788 562189 (fax); www.counselling.co.uk; bac@bac.co.uk

Kidscape (bullying/child safety), 2 Grosvenor Gardens, London SW1W 0DH; 0207 730 3300; 0207 730 7081 (fax)

Mental Health Foundation, 20-21 Cornwall Terrace, London NW1 4QL; 0207 535 7400; 0207 535 7474 (fax); mhf@mentalhealth.org.uk; www.mentalhealth.org.uk

National Youth Advocacy Service, 1 Downham Road South, Heswall, Wirrall LT60 5RG; 0151 342 7852

Place to Be (Counselling children), Edinburgh House, 154-182 Kennington Lane, London SE11 4EZ; 0207 820 6487

Trust for the Study of Adolescence, 23 New Road, Brighton BN1 1WZ; 01273 693311; 01273 679907 (fax); publications@tsa.uk.com; www.tsa.uk.com

UNICEF, 55 Lincoln's Inn Fields, London WC2A 3NB; 0207 405 5592; 0207 405 2332 (fax); www.unicef.org.uk

VOICE (learning disability), PO Box 238, Derby DE1 9JN; 01332 519872

Witness Support Programme, Victim Support, Cranmer House, 39 Brixton Road, London SW9 6DZ; 0207 735 9166; 0207 582 5712 (fax)

Young Minds, 102-108 Clerkenwell Road, London EC1M 5SA; 0207 336 8445; 0207 336 8446 (fax)

Youth Access, 2 Taylor's Yard, 67 Alderbrook Road, London SW12 8AD; 0208 772 9900

References

Alderson, P. (1993) *Children's Consent to Surgery*. Buckingham: Open University Press.

Alderson, P. (1994) *Young People, Psychiatric Treatment and Consent*. London: Social Sciences Research Unit.

Alderson, P. and Montgomery, J. (1996) *Health Care Choices: Making Decisions with Children*. London: Institute of Public Policy Research.

Alexander, F. and Selsenick, S.T. (1967) *The History of Psychiatry*. London: Allen and Unwin.

Allen, N. (1992) *Making Sense of the Children Act*. 2nd edn. London: Longman.

Alvarez, A. (1992) *Live Company: Psychoanalytic Psychotherapy with Autistic, Borderline, Deprived and Abused Children*. London: Routledge.

American Psychiatric Association (1994) *Diagnostic Criteria* from DSM-IV. Washington, DC: American Psychiatric Association.

Arnstein, S. (1969) 'A ladder of citizen participation', *Journal of the American Institute of Planners*, 35 (4): 216–24.

Association of Child Psychotherapists (nd) *Code of Professional Conduct and Ethics*. London: Association of Child Psychotherapists.

Association of Colleges (1996) *Circular 13/96: Child Protection Procedures*. London: Colleges Employers Forum.

Axline, V. (1947) *Play Therapy*. New York: Ballantine.

Axline, V. (1973) *Dibs: In Search of Self*. Harmondsworth: Penguin.

Bainham, A. (1994) '"See you in court, Mum": children as litigants', *Journal of Child Law*, 6 (3): 127–31.

Bainham, A. (1996) 'Sex education: A family lawyer's perspective', in N. Harris (ed.), *Children, Sex Education and the Law*. London: National Children's Bureau. pp. 24–44.

Bell, S. (1988) *When Salem Came to the Boro*. London: Pan.

Beloff QC, M. and Mountfield, H. (1994) *Joint Opinion: Sex Education in Schools*. London: Association of Teachers and Lecturers.

Berger, N. (1974) *Rights*. Harmondsworth: Penguin.

Bollas, C. and Sundelson, D. (1995) *The New Informants: Betrayal of Confidentiality in Psychoanalysis and Psychotherapy*. London: Karnac Books.

Bond, T. (1992) 'Ethical issues in counselling in education', *British Journal of Guidance and Counselling*, 20 (1): 51–63.

Bond, T. (1993) *Standards and Ethics for Counselling in Action*. London: Sage.

Bond, T. (1998) *BAC Guidelines: Confidentiality, Counselling and the Law*. Rugby: British Association for Counselling.

Bond, T. (1999) Personal communication.

Bovair, K. and McLaughlin, C. (1994) *Counselling in Schools: a Reader*. London: David Fulton.

Bremner, J. and Hillin, A. (1993) *Sexuality, Young People and Care: Creating a Positive Context for Training, Policy and Development*. London: Central Council for Education and Training in Social Work, London and SE Region.

Breuer, J. and Freud, S. (1985/1991) *Studies in Hysteria*. Penguin Freud Library, vol. 3. Harmondsworth: Penguin.

British Association for Counselling (1998a) *BAC Guidelines for Good Practice: Counselling in Schools*. Rugby: British Association for Counselling.

British Association for Counselling (1998b) *Code of Ethics and Practice for Counsellors*. Rugby: British Association for Counselling.

British Confederation of Psychotherapists (nd) *Code of Ethics*. London: British Confederation of Psychotherapists.

British Medical Association, General Medical Services Committee, Health Education Authority, Brook Advisory Centres, Family Planning Association and Royal College of General Practitioners (1993) *Confidentiality and People Under 16*. London: British Medical Association.

British Psychological Society (1995) *Code of Conduct, Ethical Principles and Guidelines*. London: British Psychological Society.

Butler-Sloss, E. (1988) *Report of the Inquiry into Child Abuse in Cleveland 1987*. Cm 412. London: HMSO.

Callias, M. (1992) 'Evaluation of interventions with children and adolescents', in D. Lane and A. Miller (eds), *Child and Adolescent Therapy: a Handbook*. Buckingham: Open University Press. pp. 39–64.

Callias, M., Miller, A., Lane, D. and Lanyado, M. (1992) 'The changing agenda', in D. Lane and A. Miller (eds), *Child and Adolescent Therapy: a Handbook*. Buckingham: Open University Press. pp. 3–38.

Carolin, B. (1995) 'Working with children in a family and divorce centre', *Counselling*, 6 (3): 207–10.

Casement, P. (1985) *On Learning from the Patient*. London: Tavistock.

Casemore, R. (1995) *Confidentiality and School Counselling*. Counselling in Education, Occasional Paper No. 1. Rugby: Counselling in Education/British Association for Counselling.

Cattanach, A. (1995) *Play Therapy with Abused Children*. London: Jessica Kingsley.

Children's Legal Centre, (1989a) *Childright*, 58: 11–14.

Children's Legal Centre, (1989b) *Childright*, 59: 19–20.

Children's Legal Centre (1987) *Education Rights Handbook*. London: Children's Legal Centre.

Children's Legal Centre (1994a) 'Who can young people talk to?', *Childright*, 111: 15–17.

Children's Legal Centre (1994b) *Mental Health Handbook*. 2nd edn. London: Children's Legal Centre.

Children's Legal Centre (1997) 'Offering children confidentiality: law and guidance', *Childright*, 142: 1–8.

Cobley, C. (1998) 'Financial compensation for victims of child abuse', *Journal of Social Welfare and Family Law*, 20 (3): 221–35.

Coles, R. (1998) *The Moral Intelligence of Children*. London: Bloomsbury.

Copley, B. and Forryan, B. (1997) *Therapeutic Work with Children and Young People*. 2nd edn. London: Cassell.

Cowie, H. and Pecherek, A. (1994) *Counselling: Approaches and Issues in Education*. London: David Fulton.

Crompton, M. (1992) *Counselling and Children*. London: Edward Arnold.

Crown Prosecution Service (1999) *Pre-Trial Therapy for Child Witnesses: Current Good Practice Guidance (Draft)*. York: Crown Prosecution Service.

Daniluk, J. and Haverkamp, B. (1993) 'Ethical issues in counselling adult survivors of incest', *Journal of Counseling and Development*, 72: 16–22.

D'Arcy, M. and Gosling, P. (1998) *Abuse of Trust: Frank Beck and the Leicestershire Children's Homes Scandal*. London: Bowerdean.

de Cruz, P. (1987) 'Parents, doctors and children: The *Gillick* case and beyond', *Journal of Social Welfare Law*, 2: 93–108.

De Mause, L. (1991) 'The evolution of childhood', in L. De Mause (ed.), *The History of Childhood*. London: Bellew. pp. 1–73.

Department for Education (DfE) (1994) *Education Act 1993: Sex Education in Schools*. Circular 5/94. London: Department for Education.

Department for Education and Employment (DfEE) (1995) *Protecting Children from Abuse: the Role of the Education Service*. Circular 10/95. London: Department for Education and Employment.

Department for Education and Employment (DfEE) (1998) *Protecting Young People: Good Practice in Drug Education in Schools and the Youth Service*. London: Department for Education and Employment.

Department of Environment (DoE) (1988) Circular 12/88. Department of Environment.

Department of Education and Science (DES) (1987) *Sex Education at School*. Circular 11/87. London: Department of Education and Science.

Department of Education and Science (DES) (1988) *Working Together for the Protection of Children from Abuse: Procedures within the Education Service*. Circular 4/88. London: Department of Education and Science.

Department of Health (1991a) *Children Act 1989: Guidance and Regulations, vol. 2, Family Support, Day Care and Educational Provision for Young Children*. London: HMSO.

Department of Health (1991b) *Children Act 1989: Guidance and Regulations, vol. 3, Family Placement*. London: HMSO.

Department of Health (1994) *Health and Personal Social Services Statistics*. London: HMSO.

Department of Health (1995) *Child Protection: Messages from Research*. London: HMSO.

Department of Health and Social Security (1985) *Review of Child Care Law*. London: HMSO.

Department of Health/Welsh Office (1996) *Adoption: A Service for Children (Adoption Bill – A Consultative Paper)*. London: Department of Health/Welsh Office.

Department of Health/Welsh Office (1997) *Social Services: Achievement and Challenge*. Cm 3588. London: Stationery Office.

Department of Health/Welsh Office (1999) *Mental Health Act 1983: Code of Practice*. London: Stationery Office.

Dockar-Drysdale, B. (1993) *Therapy and Consultation in Child Care*. London: Free Association.

Downey, J. (1996) 'Psychological counselling of children and young people', in R. Woolfe and W. Dryden (eds), *Handbook of Counselling Psychology*. London: Sage. pp. 308–33.

Dryden, W. (1997) *Therapists' Dilemmas*. 2nd edn. London: Sage.

Erikson, E. (1973) *Childhood and Society*. Harmondsworth: Penguin.

Fennell, P. (1992) 'Informal compulsion: the psychiatric treatment of juveniles under common law', *Journal of Social Welfare and Family Law*, 4: 311–33.

Fennell, P. (1996) *Treatment Without Consent: Law, Psychiatry and the Treatment of Mentally Disordered People since 1845*. London: Routledge.

Flekkoy, M.G. (1991) *A Voice for Children: Speaking Out as their Ombudsman*. London: UNICEF/Jessica Kingsley.

Fortin, J. (1999) *Children's Rights and the Developing Law*. London: Butterworths.

Foucault, M. (1975) *Madness and Civilisation: a History of Insanity in the Age of Reason*. London: Tavistock.

Frantz, C. (1997) 'Re C (a Minor) – Is forcible detention of a young person through the court's common law inherent jurisdiction acceptable action?', *Childright*, 136: 18–20.

Freeman, C. (1993) 'Personality disorders', in R. Kendall and A. Zealley (eds), *Companion to Psychiatric Studies*. 5th edn. London: Churchill Livingstone. pp. 587–615.

Freeman, M. (1983) *The Rights and Wrongs of Children*. London: Pinter.

Freeman, M. (1989) 'Principles and processes of the law in child protection', in W. Stainton Rogers, D. Hevey and E. Ash (eds), *Child Abuse and Neglect*. London: Batsford/Open University Press. pp. 129–35.

Freud Museum (1993) *Anna Freud*. Freud Museum Publications: London.

Friel QC, J. (1998a) 'The impact of the European Convention on Human Rights on UK Education Law', *Childright*, 143: 6–7.

Friel QC, J. (1998b) 'In the matter of the British Asssociation for Counselling, the Association for Student Counselling and the Association of Colleges'. Unpublished legal opinion obtained by the British Association for Counselling.

Freud, A. (1966) *Normality and Pathology in Childhood*. London: Hogarth.

Freud, S. (1896/1966) 'The aetiology of hysteria', *Standard Edition Complete Works*, vol. 3. London: Hogarth/Institute of Psychoanalysis.

Freud, S. (1909/1977) 'Analysis of a phobia in a five year old boy: "Little Hans"', *Case Histories 1*. Penguin Freud Library, vol. 8. Harmondsworth: Penguin.

Freud, S. (1914/1986) 'The history of the psychoanalytic movement', in *Historical and Expository Works on Psychoanalysis*. Penguin Freud Library, vol. 15. Harmondsworth: Penguin.

Freud, S. (1917/1973) *Introductory Lectures on Psychoanalysis*. Penguin Freud Library, vol. 2. Harmondsworth: Penguin.

Freud, S. (1926/1991) 'Inhibitions, symptoms and anxiety', in *On Psychopathology*. Penguin Freud Library, vol. 10. Harmondsworth: Penguin.

Freud, S. (1926/1986) 'The question of lay analysis', in *Historical and Expository Works on Psychoanalysis*. Penguin Freud Library, vol. 15. Harmondsworth: Penguin.

Freud, S. (1938/1940) *An Outline of Psycho-Analysis*. New York: Norton.

Geldard, K. and Geldard, D. (1997) *Counselling Children*. London: Sage.

Ginsberg, H. and Opper, S. (1969) *Piaget's Theory of Intellectual Development: An Introduction*. Englewood Cliffs, NJ: Prentice-Hall.

Glover, E. (1933) 'Book review', *International Journal of Psycho-Analysis* 14: 119–29.

Gomien, D. (1991) *Short Guide to the European Convention on Human Rights*. Strasbourg: Council of Europe.

Grosskurth, P. (1987) *Melanie Klein*. London: Karnac.

Gunn, M. (1996) *Sex and the Law*. 4th edn. London: Family Planning Association.

Hansard (1989) House of Lords Debates, vol. 502, No 7, Col 488.

Hansard (1993) Standing Committee, Education Bill 1992–93, 9 February, Cols 1511–16.

Hardyment, C. (1983) *Dream Babies: Child Care from Locke to Spock*. London: Jonathon Cape.

Harper, P. (1994) 'A spectrum of psychological therapies for children', in P. Clarkson and M. Pokorny (eds), *The Handbook of Psychotherapy*. London: Routledge. pp. 158–71.

Harris, N. (1996) 'The regulation and control of sex education', in N. Harris (ed.), *Children, Sex Education and the Law*. London: National Children's Bureau. pp. 1–23.

Harrison, H. (1994) 'Childline UK: how children and young people communicate their experiences by telephone', in V. Sinason (ed.), *Treating Survivors of Satanist Abuse*. London: Routledge. pp. 171–3.

Hart, R.A. (1992) *Children's Participation: from Tokenism to Citizenship*. (Innocenti Essays, 4.) Florence, Italy: UNICEF.

Hill, J. (1994) *Person-centred Approaches in Schools*. Manchester: Person Centred Counselling Services.

Home Office/Department of Health (1991) *Working Together Under the Children Act 1989: a Guide to Arrangements for Inter-Agency Cooperation for the Protection of Children from Abuse*. London: HMSO.

Home Office/Department of Health (1992) *Memorandum of Good Practice on Video Recorded Interviews with Child Witnesses in Criminal Proceedings*. London: HMSO.

Houghton-James, H. (1994) 'Children divorcing their parents', *Journal of Social Welfare and Family Law*, 2: 185–99.

House of Commons (1984) Second Report from the Social Services Committee, Session 1983–84, *Children in Care*, vol. I. London: HMSO.

Ivey, A. and Ivey, M. (1990) 'Assessing and facilitating children's cognitive development: Development and therapy in a case of child abuse', *Journal of Counseling and Development*, 68: 299–305.

Jackson, V. (1996) *Racism and Child Protection: the Black Experience of Child Sexual Abuse*. London: Cassell.

James, M. and Jongeward, D. (1975) *The People Book: Transactional Analysis for Students*. London: Addison-Wesley.

Jeffs, T. (1995) 'Children's educational rights in a new ERA?', in B. Franklin (ed.), *Handbook of Children's Rights: Comparative Policy and Practice*. London: Routledge. pp. 25–39.

Jenkins, P. (1993a) *Children's Rights*. Harlow: Longman.

Jenkins, P. (1993b) 'Counselling and the Children Act 1989', *Counselling*, 4 (4): 274–6.

Jenkins, P. (1995) 'Advocacy and the 1989 United Nations Convention on the Rights of the Child', in J. Dalrymple and J. Evans (eds), *Having a Voice*. London: Venture. pp. 31–52.

Jenkins, P. (1997a) *Counselling, Psychotherapy and the Law*. London: Sage.

Jenkins, P. (1997b) 'Prolonging the agony', *Counselling News*, 30: 16–17.

Jezzard, R. (1994) 'Adolescent psychotherapy', in P. Clarkson and M. Pokorny (eds), *The Handbook of Psychotherapy*. London: Routledge. pp. 198–207.

Jones, A.E. (1945) *Juvenile Delinquency and the Law*. Harmondsworth: Penguin.

Jones, E. (1964) *The Life and Work of Sigmund Freud*. Harmondsworth: Penguin

Kahr, B. (1996) *D.W. Winnicott: A Biographical Portrait*. London: Karnac.

Karon, B. (1987) 'Current misconceptions about psychotherapy with schizophrenics', *Dynamic Psychotherapy*, 5 (1).

Kennedy, R. (1997) *Child Abuse, Psychotherapy and the Law*. London: Free Association Books.

Kirkwood, A. (1993) *The Leicestershire Inquiry 1992*. Derby: Leicestershire County Council.

Klein, M. (1932) *The Psycho-analysis of Children*. London: Hogarth.

Lang, P. (1999) 'Counselling, counselling skills and encouraging people to talk: clarifying and addressing confusion', *British Journal of Guidance and Counselling*, 27 (1): 26–33.

Langs, R. (1979) *The Therapeutic Environment*. New York: Aronson.

Langs, R. (1988) *A Primer of Psychotherapy*. New York: Gardner.

Lansdown, G. (1995) *Taking Part: Children's Participation in Decision Making*. London: Institute for Public Policy Research.

Le Boit, J. (1979) *The Technical Problem with the Borderline Patient*. London: Aronson.

Levine, M., Doueck, H.J., with Anderson, E.M., Chavez, F.T., Deisz, R.L., George, N.A., Sharma, A., Steinberg, K.L. and Wallach, L. (1995) *The Impact of Mandated Reporting on the Therapeutic Process: Picking up the Pieces*. London: Sage.

Levy, A. and Kahan, B. (1991) *The Pindown Experience and the Protection of Children: the Report of the Staffordshire Child Care Enquiry 1990*. Stafford: Staffordshire County Council.

Lewis, A. (1992) 'The background to working in partnership', in J. Thoburn (ed.), *Participation in Practice – Involving Families in Child Protection*. Norwich: University of East Anglia. pp. 1–5.

Lyon, C. and Parton, N. (1995) 'Children's rights and the Children Act 1989', in B. Franklin (ed.), *Handbook of Children's Rights: Comparative Policy and Practice*. London: Routledge. pp. 40–55.

McLaughlin, C. (1999) 'Counselling in schools: looking back and looking forward', *British Journal of Guidance and Counselling*, 27 (1): 13–22.

McWhirter, E.H. (1991) 'Empowerment in counseling', *Journal of Counseling and Development*, 69: 222–7.

Mabey, J. and Sorensen, B. (1995) *Counselling for Young People*. Buckingham: Open University Press.

MacDonald, M. (1998) 'Spitting image', *Observer*, 30 August, p. 8.

Malek, M. (1991) *Psychiatric Admissions: a Report on Young People Entering Residential Psychiatric Care*. London: Children's Society.

Malek, M. (1993) *Passing the Buck: a Summary of Institutional Responses to Controlling Children with Difficult Behaviour*. London: Children's Society.

Masson, J. (1985a) *The Assault on Truth: Freud's Suppression of the Seduction Theory*. Harmondsworth: Penguin.

Masson, J. (1985b) *The Complete Letters of Sigmund Freud to Wilhelm Fliess 1887–1904*. London: Harvard University Press.

Miller, A. (1991) *For Your Own Good*. London: Pluto.

Morrison, B. (1997) *As If: a Quest for the 'Why' of the Killing of James Bulger*. London: Granta.

Mulholland, M. (1993) 'Re W (a Minor): autonomy, consent and the anorectic teenager', *Professional Negligence*, 9 (1): 21–4.

National Children's Home: Action for Children (NCH) (1994) *Messages from Children: Children's Evaluations of the Professional Response to Child Sexual Abuse*. London: National Children's Home.

National Society for the Prevention of Cruelty to Children (NSPCC) (1993) *The Child Witness Pack: Helping Children to Cope*. London: National Society for the Prevention of Cruelty to Children.

Noonan, E. (1983) *Counselling Young People*. London: Methuen.

Office for National Statistics (ONS) (1997) *Social Trends*. London: Stationery Office.

Parkin, A. (1999) 'Mental Health Act Code of Practice: consent of 16- and 17-year olds to admission and treatment', *Psychiatric Bulletin*, 23: 587–9.

Passey, M. (1994) 'Analytical psychotherapy with children', in P. Clarkson and M. Pokorny (eds), *The Handbook of Psychotherapy*. London: Routledge. pp. 173–94.

Pearce, J. (1994) 'Consent to treatment during childhood', *British Journal of Psychiatry*, 165: 713–16.

Plotnikoff, J. (1990) 'Compensation and child abuse', *Journal of Law and Practice*, 1 (3): 18–34.

Plotnikoff, J. and Woolfson, R. (1995) *Prosecuting Child Abuse: an Evaluation of the Government's Speedy Progress Policy*. London: Blackstone.

Plotnikoff, J. and Woolfson, R. (1996) *Children in Court*. London: Victim Support.

Ramsay, I. (1992) 'Teachers' liability: The standard of care', *Professional Negligence*, 8 (1): 6–10.

Rayment, B. (1996) *Confidential: Developing Confidentiality Policies in Youth Counselling and Advisory Services*. London: Youth Access.

Reder, P., Duncan, S. and Gray, M. (1993) *Beyond Blame: Child Abuse Tragedies Revisited*. London: Routledge.

Richardson, S. and Bacon, H. (1991) *Child Sexual Abuse: Whose Problem?* Birmingham: Venture.

Rodriguez, L. (1999) *Psychoanalysis with Children: History, Theory and Practice*. London: Free Association Books.

Roth, A., Fonagy, P., Parry, G., Target, M. and Woods, R. (1996) *What Works for Whom? a Critical Review of Psychotherapy Research*. London: Guilford.

Sanders, P. (1997) *First Steps in Counselling*. 2nd edn. Ross-on-Wye: Person Centred Counselling Services.

Schofield, G. and Thoburn, J. (1996) *Child Protection: the Voice of the Child in Decision Making*. London: Institute for Public Policy Research.

Schur, M. (1972) *Freud, Living and Dying*. New York: International Universities Press.

Segal, H. (1986) *Introduction to the Work of Melanie Klein*. London: Hogarth.

Shield, J.P.H. and Baum, J.D. (1994) 'Children's consent to treatment', *British Medical Journal*, 308: 1182–3.

Sinason, V. (1992) *Mental Handicap and the Human Condition: New Approaches from the Tavistock*. London: Free Association Books.

Smith, G. (1995) *The Protector's Handbook*. London: Women's Press.

Social Services Inspectorate (1994) *The Child, the Court and the Video: a Study of the Implementation of the Memorandum of Good Practice on Video Interviewing of Child Witnesses*. London: Department of Health.

Stainton Rogers, W. and Roche, J. (1994) *Children's Welfare and Children's Rights: a Practical Guide to the Law*. London: Hodder and Stoughton.

Strachey, J. (1934) 'The nature of the therapeutic action of psychoanalysis', *International Journal of Psychoanalysis*, 15: 127–59.

Thane, P. (1981) 'Childhood in history', in M. King (ed.), *Childhood, Welfare and Justice*. London: Batsford. pp. 6–25.

Thompson, A. (1990) *Guide to Ethical Practice in Psychotherapy*. New York: Wiley.

Thomson, R. (1996) 'Sex education and the law: working towards good practice', in N. Harris (ed.), *Children, Sex Education and the Law*. London: National Children's Bureau. pp. 99–112.

Tsiantis, J., Sandler, A.M., Anastasopoulos, D. and Markindale, B. (1996) *Countertransference in Psychoanalytic Psychotherapy with Children and Adolescents*. London: Karnac.

Tyson, P. (1980) 'The gender of the analyst', *Psychoanalytic Study of the Child*, 35: 321–38.

UNICEF (1989) *The United Nations Convention on the Rights of the Child*. London: Children's Rights Development Unit.

UNICEF (1992) *The State of the World's Children*. Oxford: Oxford University Press.

UNICEF (1993) *The State of the World's Children*. Oxford: Oxford University Press.

United Kingdom Council for Psychotherapy (1998) *Ethical Guidelines of the UKCP*. London: United Kingdom Council for Psychotherapy.

Urwin, J. (1992) 'Re R: The resurrection of parental powers?', *Professional Negligence*, 8 (2): 69–73.

Wattam, C. (1999) 'Confidentiality and the social organisation of telling', in N. Parton and C. Wattam (eds), *Child Sexual Abuse: Responding to the Experiences of Children*. Chichester: Wiley. pp. 71–89.

Weisz, J. and Weisz, B. (1993) 'Effects of psychotherapy with children and adolescents', *Developmental Clinical Psychology and Psychiatry*, 27.

Weithorn, L.A. and Campbell, S.B. (1982) 'Informed consent for treatment: An empirical study of children's capacities', *Child Development*, 53: 413–25.

Whitney, B. (1994) *The Children Act and Schools: a Guide to Good Practice*. London: Kogan Page.

Williams, R. and Morgan, H. (1994) *Suicide Prevention: the Challenge Confronted*. NHS Advisory Service Thematic Review. London: National Health Service.

Wilson, K., Kendrick, P. and Ryan, V. (1992) *Play Therapy: a Non-Directive Approach for Children and Adolescents*. London: Bailliere-Tindall.

Winnicott, D. (1965) *The Maturational Process and the Facilitating Environment*. London: Hogarth.

Winnicott, D. (1974) *Playing and Reality*. Harmondsworth: Penguin.

Winnicott, D. (1977) *The Piggle*. London: Hogarth.

Winnicott, D. (1986) *Home is Where We Start From*. Harmondsworth: Penguin.

Wolff, S. (1993) 'Personality disorders in children', in P. Tyrer and G. Stein (eds), *Personality Disorder Revisited*. London: Gaskell. pp. 64–89.

World Health Organisation (WHO) (1992) *ICD–10: Classification of Mental and Behavioural Disorders*. Geneva: World Health Organisation.

Index